NO MORE EMPTY CALORIES!

Make your calories count with delicious nutrient-dense desserts that can be everyday treats! Whether you're weight-watching, diabetic, or following a low-fat, low-cholesterol diet, here are desserts to satisfy the most demanding sweet tooth! Even your dentist will approve of hazelnut biscotti . . . elegant berries in balsamic vinegar . . . raspberries Romanoff . . . chocolate-covered fruit party platter . . . clementine soufflé . . . gingered pumpkin flan (looks and tastes like crustless pumpkin pie!) . . . mocha mousse parfait . . . Irish soda bread . . . blackberry-peach sherbet and strawberry ice milk. Try them—you'll love them—*and* the fabulous cookbook that was created for health-conscious dessert lovers everywhere!

THE ALL-NATURAL SUGAR-FREE DESSERT COOKBOOK

D0002754

THE

ALL-NATURAL
SUGAR-FREE
DESSERT
COOKBOOK

LINDA ROMANELLI LEAHY

Introduction by Elliot J. Rayfield, M.D.

A LYNN SONBERG BOOK

Published by
Dell Publishing
a division of
Bantam Doubleday Dell Publishing Group, Inc.
666 Fifth Avenue
New York, New York 10103

The reader should bear in mind that this book is not intended for the purpose of self-diagnosis or self-treatment. He or she should consult appropriate medical professionals regarding all health problems and before making any major dietary changes.

ISBN: 0-440-21100-X

Published by arrangement with Lynn Sonberg Book Services:
166 East 56 Street, 3-C, New York, NY 10022.

Printed in the United States of America

Published simultaneously in Canada

August 1992

10 9 8 7 6 5 4 3 2 1

RAD

Contents

The Ultimate Baked Apple
Chocolate-Coated Fruit Party Platter

Acknowledgments

I'm grateful to the many people who, by agreeing to participate in an informal "taste panel," helped make this cookbook a reality. Their feedback—both positive and negative—was invaluable.

I would especially like to thank: Marilyn Larkin, for her invaluable contributions to Chapter 1; Connie Costagliola, my kitchen assistant and partner in fun; my neighbors, Myron and Marion Greenstone, whose taste buds were at times pushed to the limit; Uncle Mike, who is diabetic (his words "This is too sweet, baby!" were music to my ears); Jay Cohen, my hairstylist, and all his customers who offered comments on the desserts; Lee Seifman, writer and friend, who typed the manuscript; and Connie Welch, food editor at *Weight Watchers Magazine,* who opened her library doors to me.

Thanks also to friends and family members who were valiantly objective in their taste-testing, especially Linda Mitchell-Kemp, Andrew Ramer, Pat Costa, Lynn Stallworth, Valerie Moolman, my daughters, Kate and Jenna, and my husband, Rob, who is unfailingly honest and always supportive.

Introduction

This book offers a most welcome and much needed alternative to the preparation of traditionally rich desserts. Not only are the recipes sugar free, the majority are also low in calories and fat and provide generous amounts of fiber, vitamins, and minerals. In addition to using no table sugar, the many tempting cakes, pastries, cookies, fruit desserts, pies, puddings, and frozen desserts in this collection are prepared without honey, molasses, or artificial sweeteners of any kind. This is a tremendous boon to my diabetic patients—and to all who wish to limit the amount of sugar in their family's diet. Adding to the usefulness of this collection, each dessert has been analyzed for nutrient content. The number of calories, grams of carbohydrate, fat, and cholesterol in each serving are included for easy reference. The Diabetic Exchanges, equivalent to the Dietetic Exchanges used in many weight-loss programs, are also given.

Most desserts are a nutritional indulgence, but these are genuinely good for you—the majority even conform to the healthy-eating guidelines recommended by health authorities. Low-fat recipes—three-quarters of the recipes in the book—are grouped together and can be eaten often.

Although I specialize in the treatment of diabetes in my

·medical practice, I believe *The All-Natural Sugar-Free Dessert Cookbook* will provide enjoyment to a variety of dessert lovers, whether you are interested in losing weight or following a low-fat, low-cholesterol diet; whether you or someone you love has diabetes; or whether you are simply interested in delicious desserts that are healthful enough for your family to enjoy every day and elegant enough to serve to guests on special occasions.

Why Sugarless Desserts?

Americans consume entirely too much sugar—approximately 25 percent of daily calories, according to recent studies. Of this amount, about 3 percent comes from sugars that are naturally present in fruits and vegetables; another 3 percent comes from lactose (a form of sugar) in dairy products; while *close to 20 percent of calories in our food supply comes from sugars added to foods during processing and cooking, and at the table.*

What does this mean in real numbers? If the average woman takes in 1,500 to 2,000 calories daily, 300 to 400 of those calories come from added sugar—much of which appears in desserts. This level of sugar consumption can have a negative effect on health, for the following reasons.

Sugary Desserts Have Low Nutrient Density

A food containing few nutrients and many calories is less nutrient-dense (and therefore less nutritious) than one that contains many nutrients and is low in calories. Many sugar-laden desserts are low in nutrients; for example, cakes and pies made from little more than flour, fat, and sugar have virtually nothing to offer the body beyond calories. Other foods, such as citrus fruits that are rich in vitamin C and fiber, are nutrient-dense: they provide good nutritional value for the calories they contain.

Many of the desserts in this book are more nutrient-dense than their prepackaged or traditionally prepared counterparts. For example, the Sesame-Oat Cookies (p. 61) are made from rolled oats, nonfat dry milk, all-natural peanut butter, and sesame seeds—good sources of protein, vitamins, and minerals; in many store-bought varieties of oat cookies, the first few ingredients (which are the most plentiful) listed on the package are white flour, oil, and sugar. Strawberry Cheesecake Cups made with yogurt cheese (p. 27), Oat Bran Macaroons made with unprocessed oat bran (p. 43), and Raspberries Romanoff made with nonfat yogurt (p. 82) are just a few of the many other healthful, nutrient-dense desserts offered here.

Sugar Consumption Is Linked with Obesity

From a health standpoint, one of the primary drawbacks of consuming too many sugary foods of low nutrient density is that you eat them *instead of* nonsugary, nutrient-dense foods. When this happens, good nutrition can suffer at the same time obesity can develop.

There are several reasons for this. Because sugar is absorbed so quickly it tends to increase a food's caloric value without increasing the feeling of "fullness" you get from consuming it. You enjoy the taste, so you keep on eating, unwittingly taking in more calories than you need. Could you eat the same amount of calories you get from a high-sugar dessert in the form of nutrient-dense foods, such as fruits and grains? Highly unlikely, since the nutrient-dense foods are bulky and filling, as well as nutritious. You're bound to feel "stuffed" way before you overindulge.

In some people, eating a sugary food may trigger a desire to eat more and more sugary foods. This, unfortunately, is a trap: you're apt to forgo healthful foods in favor of high-sugar fare and, over time, cause your diet to become seriously unbalanced. Meanwhile, all those sugary foods can contribute to your becoming overweight.

Finally, if you allow sugar-laden desserts and snacks to replace nourishing foods in your diet, your body will continue to crave the nutrients it needs. You may find yourself eating large amounts of food in an effort to maintain or reestablish health—and piling on pounds in the process.

Sugar Consumption Can Become a Lifelong Habit

Although there is no evidence to support the idea that sugar is addictive (i.e., that it causes physical dependence or triggers withdrawal symptoms when its use is abruptly halted), eating sugary foods *can* become habit-forming—and therefore potentially harmful to health.

Human beings are born with an innate liking for sweet-tasting foods, so we're already predisposed to enjoy whatever sugar-containing items we eat. Of course, our sweet tooth is perfectly capable of being satisfied by the taste of ripe, juicy fruit—but several factors conspire against our satisfying it in this way.

For one thing, we're surrounded by advertisements displaying rich desserts of all kinds, which subconsciously create a desire in us for these types of foods. And peer pressure—watching everyone around us eating cakes and custards, for example—also exerts a powerful force on what we feel as though *we* want to eat. As a result, it may be difficult to conceive of craving an apple, for instance, rather than an apple turnover. That's why the Apple Turnovers recipe on p. 115, which uses ripe apples and apple butter as sweeteners, is a helpful option for people who want to limit their sugar intake without forgoing the desserts we're used to having as part of the American diet.

Even if your ultimate goal is to wean yourself away from sweet desserts entirely, you'll most likely need to take interim steps. These would include preparing your favorite desserts using fruit—not sugar—as a sweetener. That way, you give yourself and your family time to acclimate your taste buds to a different kind of sweetness.

Sugar Consumption Is Associated with Certain Diseases

Sugar alone won't cause disease. But too much sugar in the diet, in combination with heredity and life-style factors, may create a host of adverse effects in the body. As we've seen, overconsumption of sugar can lead to obesity, which, in turn, is a risk factor in heart disease, high blood pressure, and gallstones. Overweight individuals are also relatively more likely to develop adult-onset diabetes (see p. xviii), and this disorder is helped when you cut back on the amount and type of sugar in your diet.

Some studies suggest that too much sugar may increase the level of blood fats such as triglycerides in susceptible individuals. If you have a high triglyceride level, one of the risk factors for heart disease, your physician may recommend that you follow a low-sugar diet.

Sugar is also linked to gastrointestinal disease in some people. Those who suffer from colitis, diverticular disease, and abdominal bloating after ingestion of sugar are often advised to follow a low-sugar, high-fiber diet.

There is no question that sugary snacks and desserts, especially when eaten alone between meals, play a role in the development of tooth decay. Sticky and caramelized forms of sugar, which adhere to the teeth, are the types most likely to cause dental problems.

Finally, people who are prone to acne outbreaks and pimply skin may wish to cut back on sugary desserts and concentrate on following a balanced diet. This strategy often leads to improvement in skin and overall health.

Sugar Consumption Can Give You a "High"—and Low

The term *sugar high* generally refers to the quick burst of energy you experience when you eat a concentrated simple sugar—a candy bar or other snack made primarily of table sugar—on an empty stomach. What you're really feeling is a rapid, dramatic rise in blood glucose (the digested form of sugar). Your pancreas responds (in the nondiabetic person) to this rise in glucose with a similar outpouring of insulin that brings your glucose level back to the normal range.

This rapid rise and subsequent fall of glucose in the blood has consequences. The energy "high" you experienced in the minutes following ingestion of simple sugar is followed by an energy "low" (this effect can be very pronounced in children, who react quickly and dramatically to biochemical changes in the body).

For some people, the low is accompanied by feelings of irritability, sluggishness, and overall malaise. To counteract these effects, you may decide to help yourself to yet another serving of sugar—which can lock you into a vicious cycle characterized by mood swings and alternating energy peaks and valleys.

A better strategy for maintaining energy is to eat complex carbohydrate foods, which include fruits, grain products, and vegetables. It takes time for the body to digest these foods and break them down into simpler sugars that can be absorbed into the bloodstream (a simple sugar food is *already* broken down, so its sugar rushes into the bloodstream almost instantaneously) and from there, into the cells for use as fuel. This relatively slow process permits a steady, more measured flow of sugar into the blood; you avoid energy highs and lows, keep your blood glucose level steady, and generally feel better.

Beware of "Hidden" Sugars

Sugar is known by a host of names; some may be familiar to you, while others may draw a blank. To prevent confusion, this book relies only on the natural sweetness of fruit in its various forms (see p. 2, "Types of Fruit Used in These Recipes") for the desserts.

To avoid unknowingly indulging in sugar, you should become familiar with the various ways in which it appears on food labels. Generally speaking, ingredients that end in *ose* are apt to be sugars. These include: dextrose (another name for glucose), sucrose (table sugar), high fructose corn syrups, and maltose.

Any ingredient that has the word *sugar* attached to it offers no advantages over table sugar. These include: beet sugar, brown sugar, confectioner's sugar, invert sugar, raw sugar, turbinado sugar.

Honey, molasses, and maple syrup are no better for you nutritionally than table sugar and have the same effects in the body.

Mannitol, sorbitol, and xylitol are sugar alcohol products that are absorbed less slowly into the bloodstream than sucrose or glucose. However, because they may have undesirable side effects (in large amounts, they can cause gastrointestinal discomfort and diarrhea), they are not used in these recipes.

Artificial sweeteners aren't used because we believe in using all natural products.

How Can This Book Help Diabetics?

Because many of you, like the author, may have a family member with diabetes, I believe it would be useful to spend a moment explaining why sugar-free desserts can play an important role in healthful meal-planning for diabetics.

Simply put, diabetes is a condition in which the body fails to regulate the blood glucose level properly. There are two major types of diabetes: insulin-dependent diabetes (sometimes known as "juvenile diabetes" because its onset is usually in childhood) and non-insulin-dependent diabetes (also known as "adult-onset diabetes" because it usually occurs later in life).

In insulin-dependent diabetes, the pancreas doesn't produce enough insulin to signal cells to remove glucose from the bloodstream, so insulin must be supplied in order to keep blood glucose levels in the normal range. In adult-onset diabetes, there is a modest reduction in the pancreas's ability to manufacture insulin and body cells may become insensitive to insulin. In addition, many of the cells simply don't respond normally to the message to start removing glucose from the blood.

The bottom line for both types of diabetes is that glucose has trouble getting into the cells, where it can be used as fuel, and tends to build up in the bloodstream. If a diabetic whose blood glucose level is already high consumes a simple sugar, then his blood glucose level soars—which can result in coma. Over time, diabetics may develop atherosclerosis, nerve damage, and other severe health problems. It is currently standard practice to teach all patients with insulin-dependent diabetes and many patients with non-insulin-dependent diabetes to monitor their blood sugar levels with fingerstick testing of their blood sugar levels (self–blood glucose monitoring). Many diabetes specialists and nutritionists have found striking variability in the rise in blood glucose levels in response to the identical food item and portion size from person to person. For this reason, if you have diabetes, I would urge you to follow this procedure in general and specifically when partaking of some of the desserts in this cookbook. You may be pleasantly surprised in some cases and disappointed in others. But you will have immediate feedback in regard to what the effect of any given dessert has on your blood sugar level. The only caveat is, if you are having white clam sauce with your pasta in the same meal as one of the desserts and your blood glucose soars, you won't be certain as to which food is the culprit. Then you'll have to play detective to sort things out.

Learning to Live with Less Sugar

When embarking on any major dietary change, it's important to understand that a change of attitude is also necessary. You're not depriving yourself of sugar-laden desserts; you're giving yourself the gift of potentially better health.

During the transition phase, you may think, "This needs more sugar!" Yet in less time than you might believe possible, you and your family will be on the road to *preferring* the fresh, unmasked flavor of fruit-sweetened desserts.

Give yourself time to acclimate your palate to these new taste sensations. Follow the hints for creating the sweetest possible versions of these recipes. Remember that what you lose in sugary taste, you will gain in nutritional benefits. And in time you will actually come to prefer these desserts to the unhealthful ones you are currently eating.

Elliot J. Rayfield, M.D.
Clinical Professor of Medicine
Division of Endocrinology
Mt. Sinai School of Medicine
New York, N.Y.

How to Make Great Fruit-Sweetened Desserts

Creating this sugar-free dessert book has been an exciting challenge for me. There are several diabetics in my family, and I looked forward to devising tasty desserts that would hold the same appeal as the traditionally prepared favorites they could no longer eat. I even dared hope they would come to prefer these fruit-sweetened desserts to the sugary ones they were accustomed to.

I also have very young nieces and nephews who are constantly bombarded with temptations: their friends gorge on cakes and cookies; the television programs they watch sing the praises of sugary snacks and desserts; in the supermarket, boxes of so-called goodies line the shelves and practically jump into their hands. Wouldn't it be wonderful, I thought, to present them with good-tasting alternatives to all this junk food? And, in the process, perhaps keep them from developing the kind of overly sweet tooth that could stay with them for a lifetime.

Whether or not I've succeeded in my loftier goals remains to be seen. But I do know that the cakes, cookies, puddings, pastries, and other desserts in this book were devoured quickly and enthusiastically by children and adults alike. Most important, they met my very demanding criteria: delicious taste, appealing texture, low in fat and calories.

Each recipe in this book is a labor of love. What pleases me most is knowing that the work I put into creating these recipes is what makes them so easy for you to follow—with great results!

Types of Fruit Used in These Recipes

When I was doing research for this book, I discovered that our word *fruit* comes from the Latin word *fructus,* which means "to use"; its plural form, *frui,* means "to enjoy." How perfect! In fact, fruit in all its forms has been a joy to use— and savor—in creating these naturally sweet desserts.

Fresh Fruit: Purchase your fresh fruit ripe and ready to eat: melons should be fragrant and yield to the touch; bananas should be ripe and soft. Pears are usually hard when you buy them, and may need to sit at home to ripen for three or four days to attain maximum sweetness.

Wash all fresh fruit thoroughly and pat dry before using.

If for some reason the fruit you purchased isn't as ripe as you expected, add a little fruit spread to the recipe to adjust flavor.

Unsweetened Fruit Juice: Always check the label to be sure the juice you're thinking of purchasing is unsweetened. A good source is canned fruit packed in its own juice (pour off the juice and save in the refrigerator for use in recipes).

Unsweetened Fruit Juice Concentrate: These concentrates are *much* sweeter than fruit juices; a little goes a long way! As with fruit juice, check the label to make sure the concentrate doesn't contain added sugar. Thaw the concentrate before using, and keep it covered in the refrigerator.

In my experience, grape juice concentrate adds the most sweetness with the least fruity flavor; however, your baked goods turn purple (kids may actually like this development!). You can use white grape juice, but it has a very different taste —slightly tangy, not as sweet—so try some before you use it.

Plain, unsweetened apple juice concentrate is used in all recipes calling for apple juice concentrate. Natural-style and Granny Smith unsweetened juice concentrates have decidedly different flavors; again, check for sweetness before using them.

Spreadable Fruit: These are jams, jellies, preserves, and marmalades that are either unsweetened or sweetened with fruit juice concentrates. There are a number of brands to choose from and they all vary in degrees of sweetness. The trick is to experiment. Buy a variety of brands and taste them on crackers.

In most recipes, the amount of spreadable fruit may be increased by 1 to 2 tablespoons for sweeter flavor—but this strategy also adds more fruit flavor. For sweetness with the least amount of fruit flavor, use peach or apricot spreadable fruit.

Pourable Fruit: These are fruit syrups sweetened with juice concentrates. Some have small pieces of fruit in them, which add a little texture. There are several brands on the market, and you should read labels carefully because some contain corn syrup and fructose powder.

When baking, don't interchange fruit spreads and pourable fruit. They have different consistencies, and substituting one for the other will change the texture of your batter.

Quick and Easy Desserts

When you love to bake, as I do, you can easily spend hours in the kitchen and lose all track of time. This is a wonderful experience when your time is unlimited—but for most of us, this is rarely the case. On days when you crave dessert but can only spare minutes, not hours, for preparation, choose among the following recipes. Preparation time for each is under ten minutes (actual baking time may be longer, however).

Cookies: Blackberry Stars, p. 47.

Fruit Desserts: Berries in Balsamic Vinegar, p. 65; Cranberry Grilled Grapefruit, p. 69; Grapefruit in Warm Blackberry Sauce, p. 74; Grilled Summer Figs, p. 75; Grilled Tropical Fruit with Coconut "Cream," p. 76; Fruit with Peach Custard Sauce, p. 72; Lemon-Ginger Pear Cobbler, p. 77; Melon Balls in Citrus Syrup, p. 79; Minted Peaches, p. 80; Raspberries Romanoff, p. 82.

Puddings, Custards, Mousses, Soufflés, and Compotes: Apple-Currant Compote, p. 121; Brandied Peach Sauce, p. 122; Cantaloupe Chiffon, p. 123; Caramel Custard, p. 124; Crème Fraîche, p. 151; Gingered Pumpkin Flan, p. 132.

Tea Cakes and Quick Breads: Fruit-and-Nut Crescents, p. 166; Irish Soda Bread, p. 159.

Frozen Desserts: Blackberry-Peach Sherbet, p. 175; Cherry-Banana Ice Pops, p. 177; Frozen Banana-Cinnamon Yogurt, p. 180.

Kitchen Essentials

To prepare these desserts in the quickest, easiest fashion, it helps to have all the proper tools on hand. The following items will assist you in preparing the best-quality desserts possible.

Bakeware

Bundt pan
Cake pans (round, square)
Cookie sheets
Loaf pan
Muffin pan
Pie pan
Springform pan (removable bottom)

Bakeware Accessories

Cooling rack
Custard cups
Soufflé dish

Kitchen and Pastry Tools

Cutting board
Fruit corer (to core apples and pears)
Measuring cups and spoons
Paring knife
Pastry blender
Pastry brush
Rolling pin
Ruler (to measure pie crusts and cookie squares)
Spatula
Thermometers (oven and candy)
Toothpicks or cake tester
Whisk
Zester (to peel outer rind off lemons and other fruit)

Helpful Equipment

Blender
Food processor
Ice-cream maker
Microwave oven
Mixer

Sugarless "Classics"

The traditional tastes, textures, and forms of our favorite desserts are the models against which I measured the success of my sugarless recipes. In most cases, the results were remarkably similar—despite the fact that I used no sugar and much less fat than usual. Here's a look at what to expect when you prepare these "classic" desserts in a nontraditional way.

Brownies

The typical brownie is made with lots of sugar, chocolate, and fat—and very little flour. This creates a chewy, gooey dessert. The brownies in my book have a cakier texture, and the fat comes from a no-cholesterol nut butter instead of regular butter or lard.

Cakes

Because there is no sugar and very little fat in my cake recipes the texture will be slightly different from what you're accustomed to.

For best results, be sure all ingredients are at room temperature (unless otherwise indicated) so that air can be more easily incorporated into the batter. Bake cakes in the center of the oven so that heat circulates evenly.

Compotes

Compotes are cooked fruit stews made with added sugar to create a syrupy effect. But it's really not necessary to use sugar. Instead, I add a small amount of fruit spread for texture and to heighten the already sweet flavor of the stewed fruit.

Cream Puffs

My cream puffs are virtually indistinguishable from the ones that use sugar and many more egg yolks than my recipe calls for.

Custards

Again, my custards are very close in texture—but very much lower in calories and cholesterol—to ones prepared according to traditional recipes; it's the cornstarch and gelatin that make them smooth and creamy. Although they may be slightly jiggly when they come out of the oven, these custards set nicely once they've cooled and been refrigerated.

Frozen Desserts

There's no cream of any sort in these refreshing desserts; nonfat yogurt, tofu, low-fat or nonfat milk, or buttermilk take its place. These substitutes are low in fat and calories, but a fuller-bodied texture can still be achieved, especially with the addition of one egg yolk.

Taste your mixture before pouring it into the ice-cream machine so that you can adjust the flavor and sweetness to your taste.

Mousses

I use unflavored gelatin and instant nonfat dry milk instead of heavy cream in my mousse recipes, so the result is lighter in texture than you might expect (some people actually like it better this way!).

Pies

My pie crusts are delicious but somewhat less flaky than those made with large amounts of sugar and fat. For best results, make the crust by hand, using a pastry blender or two knives to cut in the fat; or use a food processor, pulsing after you've added liquid until the dough forms.

Puddings

Forget lots of egg yolks, heavy cream, and whole milk. These puddings—cooked, uncooked, baked, microwaved, made in the saucepan or frying pan—got rave reviews! And they're all relatively low in fat and calories.

Quick Breads and Tea Cakes

These breakfast accompaniments are very close in texture to the originals but are significantly lower in fat and calories: I use reduced-calorie margarine instead of butter and very few egg yolks.

Scones

Scones are usually made with a whole stick of butter; only one half of that is used in my recipe, which serves twelve people— and results are the same as the "real" thing!

Sherbets and Sorbets

Pureed fruit is a "natural" for these sugar-free frozen desserts. There's absolutely no need to add sugar.

Soufflés

Like the mousses, my soufflés are lighter in texture and lower in fat, calories, and cholesterol—but still have a delightfully satisfying taste. My trick is to use no cream and far fewer eggs than in traditional recipes.

Waffles

I use a variety of flours, grains, nuts, and fruit in my waffles— and the results are terrific!

Helpful Hints

The following tips will assist you in creating the sweetest, most "texture-perfect" desserts possible.

Browning

Brush a little egg white on turnovers, empanadas, and other desserts to make them look more appealing. Or brush on a small amount of pourable fruit or fruit spread mixed with water.

Eggs

Eggs help incorporate air into your batter. Always use them at room temperature, since this increases their volume. If you're in a hurry to bake and the eggs are cold, place them in a bowl of warm water for ten minutes.

All recipes in this book use large eggs only.

Extracts

Use pure extracts whenever possible for better flavor and no aftertaste.

Flours

When measuring cups of flour, lightly spoon the flour into a cup and level it off with a knife. Never pack flour down, or you'll end up using much more than the recipe calls for.

Whole wheat flour tends to be dry and grainy; mixing it with other flours will improve its texture in cakes and cookies.

Have a variety of flours—all-purpose, whole wheat, buckwheat—in your pantry.

Oil

Use vegetable oil in these recipes (rapeseed oil, available under the brand name Puritan, may be your healthiest choice). Remember that there's no need to butter or grease pans before cooking or baking; use a no-fat cooking spray instead.

Toasting

To toast nuts, seeds, coconut, and grains, place them in a skillet on low heat and stir occasionally until they're lightly brown.

Vegetarian Substitutions

In recipes calling for gelatin, substitute agar flakes, following package directions.

In recipes calling for ricotta or cottage cheese, tofu may be substituted.

Read Labels

I can't overemphasize the importance of reading labels before purchasing *any* ingredient. Many manufacturers simply aren't committed to the sugar-free concept. They add high fructose corn syrup and other forms of sugar to an otherwise pure fruit product. Don't purchase these brands.

Fortunately, there are enough fruit-only products to choose from. Take the extra time you need at the beginning of your sugarless baking adventure to select the brands that contain fruit and fruit juices only.

Enjoy

These recipes have helped convince my family and friends that sugar free is *not* synonymous with drab or tasteless. Many have remarked that this new, delicious concept in dessert-making is tempting, tantalizing—and at times almost too sweet to be true! As you begin to prepare the desserts in this book, I trust you will be on the road to a similar discovery.

Abbreviations and Symbols

kcal = kilocalories
g = grams
mg = milligrams
<1 = less than 1

2

Cakes and Pastries

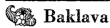 Baklava

Makes 12 servings.
A heavenly Greek dessert with layers of crisp phyllo, dried fruit,
and nuts, drenched in fruit sauce.

- 3/4 cup golden raisins
- 1/2 cup finely chopped dates
- 1/3 cup coarsely chopped walnuts
- 6 sheets thawed phyllo pastry
- 1 tablespoon margarine, melted
- 1/2 cup apricot pourable fruit
- 1/4 cup water
- 1 teaspoon fresh lemon juice

1. Preheat oven to 350°F; spray 11-× 7½-inch baking pan
   with vegetable cooking spray; set aside.

2. In medium bowl combine raisins, dates, and walnuts.

3. Cut phyllo stack in half crosswise; make one stack of 12
   sheets. (When you're working quickly, there's no need to
   cover phyllo with a damp towel.)

4. Place 3 sheets of phyllo in bottom of pan, lightly spraying
   each sheet with cooking spray. Sprinkle about 2
   tablespoons raisin mixture on top. Cover with a single
   sheet of phyllo; coat with cooking spray and sprinkle with
   raisin mixture.

5. Continue alternating with 5 more single sheets of coated
   phyllo and raisin mixture.

6. Top with triple layer of coated phyllo sheets. Press down
   edges. Stack should be about 1½ inches high. Drizzle
   with margarine.

7. Bake 25 minutes or until golden.

8. In small saucepan combine pourable fruit, water, and lemon juice; cook over medium heat until slightly thickened (about 10 minutes), stirring frequently. Pour hot syrup over pastry as soon as it is removed from oven. Cool on rack; serve at room temperature.

Per serving:
Calories: 137   Fat: 4 g   Sodium: 63 mg   Protein: 2 g
Carbohydrate: 26 g   Cholesterol: 0 mg
Diabetic exchanges:
Starch/Bread: 0.50   Fat: 0.75   Fruit: 1.25

Buckwheat-Millet Dessert Waffles

Makes 16 waffles (8 servings).
Millet adds not only crunch but fiber to these waffles. Variation: Omit cocoa powder and serve with Frozen Peach Tofu and Brandied Peach Sauce.

Batter:

1	cup unbleached all-purpose flour
3/4	cup buckwheat flour
1/4	cup millet*
2	tablespoons cocoa powder, optional
2	teaspoons baking powder
1/2	teaspoon baking soda
1/4	teaspoon salt
13/4	cups skim milk
1/4	cup vegetable oil
1/4	cup strawberry spreadable fruit
1	large egg + 2 egg whites
2	teaspoons vanilla extract

Sauce:

2	pints sliced hulled strawberries
1/2	cup orange juice
1/4	cup strawberry spreadable fruit

1. To prepare waffles, in large bowl combine dry ingredients; in 4-cup measure combine milk, oil, spreadable fruit, egg and egg whites, and vanilla extract. Stir into dry ingredients until blended. Refrigerate, covered, 15 minutes.

Note: Waffles may be frozen, reheated, or toasted.
* Available at health food stores.

2. To prepare sauce, in medium saucepan, over medium heat, combine strawberries, juice, and spreadable fruit; cook about 5 minutes, stirring occasionally until fruit spread dissolves and mixture thickens slightly. Puree in blender.

3. Preheat waffle iron; cook waffles according to manufacturer's instructions. Serve with warm sauce.

Per serving:
Calories: 288   Fat: 9 g   Sodium: 276 mg   Protein: 8 g
Carbohydrate: 45 g   Cholesterol: 28 mg
Diabetic exchanges:
Starch/Bread: 2.00   Fat: 1.75   Fruit: 1.00

Chocolate Cream Puffs

Makes 24 cream puffs.
Try these light and crispy shells with a variety of fresh fruit, yogurt, or filling of your choice selected from the frozen dessert recipes beginning on page 173.

Pastry:

- 1/2 cup reduced-calorie tub margarine
- 1/4 teaspoon brandy extract
- 13/4 cups unbleached all-purpose flour
- 1/4 teaspoon salt
- 4 large eggs

Filling:

- 1/4 cup cocoa powder
- 3 tablespoons cornstarch
- 11/2 cups skim milk
- 1/2 cup peach spreadable fruit
- 1 teaspoon vanilla extract

1. Preheat oven to 450°F; spray 2 baking sheets with vegetable cooking spray; set aside.

2. In medium saucepan combine margarine, brandy extract, and 1 cup water; bring to boil over medium-high heat. Remove from heat; stir in flour and salt all at once. Stir vigorously with wooden spoon until mixture leaves sides of pan and forms a ball.

3. Add eggs, one at a time, beating until smooth after each addition.

4. Spoon mixture into pastry bag fitted with a 1/2-inch-wide plain tip; pipe out twenty-four 2-inch rounds (or drop mixture by heaping teaspoonfuls onto prepared pans).

5. Bake 15 minutes; reduce heat to 350°F and bake 20 minutes longer. Place on rack to cool. (May be frozen until ready to use.)

6. To prepare filling, in medium saucepan combine cocoa powder and cornstarch; whisk in milk to combine; bring to boil over medium-high heat, whisking constantly. Boil 1 minute; remove from heat.

7. Whisk in spreadable fruit and vanilla until blended. Spoon into medium bowl; press plastic wrap onto surface of chocolate; refrigerate until ready to use.

8. Slit each puff in half horizontally; fill with chocolate cream.

Per serving:
Calories: 89   Fat: 3 g   Sodium: 78 mg   Protein: 3 g
Carbohydrate: 13 g   Cholesterol: 36 mg
Diabetic exchanges:
Starch/Bread: 0.50   Fat: 0.75   Fruit: 0.25

Devil's Food Cake

Makes 12 servings.
The only word to describe this cake is Yum!

- 2 cups unbleached all-purpose flour
- 1/3 cup cocoa powder
- 1 teaspoon baking soda
- 1/4 teaspoon salt
- 1 cup apricot pourable fruit
- 3/4 cup low-fat buttermilk
- 1/4 cup reduced-calorie tub margarine, melted and cooled
- 3 large eggs at room temperature, lightly beaten
- 2 teaspoons vanilla extract

1. Preheat oven to 350°F; spray 9-cup Bundt pan with vegetable cooking spray; set aside.

2. In food processor fitted with steel blade, combine flour, cocoa, baking soda, and salt; add remaining ingredients and pulse until combined, scraping down sides of bowl.

3. Pour batter into prepared pan; bake 35 minutes or until toothpick inserted in center comes out clean.

4. Cool on rack 15 minutes; remove from pan and cool completely.

Per serving:
Calories: 175   Fat: 4 g   Sodium: 199 mg   Protein: 5 g
Carbohydrate: 30 g   Cholesterol: 54 mg
Diabetic exchanges:
Starch/Bread: 1.00   Meat, Lean: 0.25   Fat: 0.67   Fruit: 1.00

Fruit Cocktail Cheesecake

Makes 8 servings.
This is a light cheesecake that's picture perfect.

- 3 cups part-skim ricotta cheese
- 1 can (16 ounces) unsweetened juice-packed fruit cocktail
- 2 large eggs + 2 egg whites, lightly beaten
- 1/2 cup low-fat buttermilk
- 1/2 cup unbleached all-purpose flour
- 1/4 cup apricot spreadable fruit
- 2 teaspoons vanilla extract
- 3/4 teaspoon ground cinnamon
- 1/2 teaspoon ground nutmeg
- 1/2 teaspoon grated lemon peel
- 1/8 teaspoon salt
- 2 tablespoons unblanched sliced almonds

1. Preheat oven to 375°F; spray 8-inch springform pan with vegetable cooking spray; set aside.

2. In large bowl combine all ingredients except slivered almonds; pour into prepared pan; sprinkle with almonds.

3. Bake 1 hour and 15 minutes, or until puffed and browned. Cool on rack 2 hours. Refrigerate 2–3 hours before serving.

Per serving:
Calories: 246   Fat: 10 g   Sodium: 198 mg
Protein: 15 g   Carbohydrate: 25 g   Cholesterol: 82 mg
Diabetic exchanges:
Starch/Bread: 0.50   Meat, Lean: 2.00   Fat: 0.75
Fruit: 1.00

Ginger Squares

Makes 9 squares.
Fresh ginger adds "zing" to these tasty cake squares.

- 1 1/2 cups unbleached all-purpose flour
- 1 teaspoon baking powder
- 1 teaspoon ground ginger
- 1/2 teaspoon baking soda
- 1/2 teaspoon grated fresh gingerroot
- 1/2 teaspoon ground cinnamon
- 2/3 cup unsweetened grape juice concentrate
- 3 tablespoons vegetable oil
- 1 large egg, lightly beaten

1. Preheat oven to 350°F; spray 8-inch-square baking pan with vegetable cooking spray; set aside.

2. In large bowl combine dry ingredients. In medium bowl combine juice concentrate, oil, and egg. Add liquid ingredients to dry; stir until just blended.

3. Spoon batter into prepared pan spreading evenly; bake 25–30 minutes or until toothpick inserted in center comes out clean. Cool on rack 10 minutes; remove from pan and cool completely. Cut into squares.

Per serving:
Calories: 174   Fat: 5 g   Sodium: 102 mg   Protein: 3 g
Carbohydrate: 28 g   Cholesterol: 24 mg
Diabetic exchanges:
Starch/Bread: 1.00   Fat: 1.00   Fruit: 1.00

Polenta-Apricot Swirl Cake

Makes 12 servings.

Cornmeal, a New World product, found its way to Europe in the sixteenth century, and is known there as polenta. The swirl top on this cake makes it pretty enough for a dinner party.

2 large egg yolks
1/4 cup apricot pourable fruit
3 tablespoons margarine, melted and cooled
2 teaspoons vanilla extract
13/4 cups finely ground cornmeal (polenta)
3/4 cup unbleached all-purpose flour
2 teaspoons baking powder
1/2 teaspoon ground nutmeg
1/4 teaspoon salt
11/2 cups 1% low-fat milk
1/4 cup apricot spreadable fruit

1. Preheat oven to 350°F; spray 9-inch-round baking pan with vegetable cooking spray; set aside.

2. In large bowl of electric mixer, beat yolks, pourable fruit, margarine, and vanilla extract at high speed 5 minutes.

3. In medium bowl combine dry ingredients; gradually add to yolk mixture at low speed, alternating with milk until well blended.

4. Spoon mixture into prepared pan; drizzle apricot in circles on batter; with a knife, swirl around into batter. Bake about 40 minutes or until toothpick inserted into center comes out clean. Cool on rack 10 minutes; remove from pan and cool completely.

Per serving:
Calories: 180   Fat: 5 g   Sodium: 171 mg   Protein: 4 g
Carbohydrate: 30 g   Cholesterol: 37 mg

Diabetic exchanges:
Starch/Bread: 1.50   Fat: 0.75   Fruit: 0.50

Strawberry Cheesecake Cups

Makes 6 cups.
Nonfat yogurt cheese is an excellent base for cheesecakes and sweet spreads.

    1 cup yogurt cheese*
    1/2 cup strawberry spreadable fruit
    1 large egg
    2 tablespoons nonfat sour cream alternative
    2 tablespoons unbleached all-purpose flour
    1 teaspoon vanilla extract
    1/8 teaspoon salt
    6 whole strawberries to garnish, optional

1. Preheat oven to 300°F; line 12 muffin cups with paper liners; set aside.

2. In food processor or blender, puree all ingredients until smooth; spoon mixture evenly into prepared muffin pan.

3. Bake 25 minutes. Cool in pan on rack. Cover and refrigerate 2 hours before serving. Garnish with strawberries.

Per serving:
Calories: 114   Fat: 1 g   Sodium: 86 mg   Protein: 4 g
Carbohydrate: 19 g   Cholesterol: 35 mg
Diabetic exchanges:
Dairy, Skim Milk: 0.50   Fat: 0.25   Fruit: 1.00

* To make yogurt cheese, line a large sieve with paper towels or place filter in top of a drip coffeemaker. Add 2 cups nonfat yogurt. Let drip, covered and refrigerated overnight.

Sweet Fig Pizza

Makes 12 servings.
This pizza dough is easy to make. An unusual and scrumptious dessert to delight family and friends.

Dough:

- 1¼ cups unbleached all-purpose flour
- 1 package active dry yeast
- ½ teaspoon salt
- 2 tablespoons apricot pourable fruit
- ¼ cup + 1 tablespoon warm water (120°–130°F)
- 1 tablespoon vegetable oil

Topping:

- 1 cup finely chopped, stemmed Calimyrna figs
- 2 tablespoons marsala wine
- ¼ teaspoon ground nutmeg
- ¼ cup apricot spreadable fruit
- 2 tablespoons chopped walnuts
- 1 teaspoon vegetable oil

1. To prepare dough, in food processor fitted with steel blade, combine flour, yeast, and salt.

2. With machine running, add spreadable fruit, then water and oil; when dough gathers into a ball, pulse 20 times to knead.

3. Spray medium bowl with vegetable cooking spray. Place dough in prepared bowl; turn to coat top surface. Cover with plastic wrap and let rise in a warm, draft-free place until doubled in size, 30–45 minutes.

4. To prepare topping, in small bowl combine figs, wine, and nutmeg; stir frequently until wine is absorbed.

5. Preheat oven to 425°F; spray 10-inch pizza pan with vegetable cooking spray.

6. Punch down dough and place in center of prepared pan. With fingers, press dough into 10-inch circle. Brush with spreadable fruit.

7. Spoon fig mixture evenly on top of pizza; sprinkle with nuts and drizzle with oil.

8. Bake 15–20 minutes until crust is brown and crisp. Serve warm or at room temperature.

Per serving:
Calories: 138   Fat: 3 g   Sodium: 96 mg   Protein: 2 g
Carbohydrate: 27 g   Cholesterol: 0 mg
Diabetic exchanges:
Starch/Bread: 0.75   Fat: 0.50   Fruit: 1.00

Please note: The remainder of the recipes in this chapter contain no added sugar, of course, but they do derive more than 35 percent of their calories from fat. While these desserts are far healthier than most traditional recipes, you may want to save them for special occasions if fat content is your primary concern.

Carrot Cake

Makes 16 servings.

Carrot cake, star of the sixties health food movement, becomes even healthier in this sugar-free, low-fat version. Frosting, although low in fat, will raise the fat gram count.

- 1 1/4 cups unbleached all-purpose flour
- 1 cup whole wheat pastry flour
- 1/4 cup sunflower seeds
- 1 teaspoon each, baking powder and baking soda
- 1/2 teaspoon ground mace
- 1/2 teaspoon ground cinnamon
- 1/2 teaspoon salt
- 1/2 cup vegetable oil
- 2 large eggs + 4 egg whites at room temperature
- 1 medium-size ripe banana, mashed
- 1/4 cup unsweetened apple juice concentrate
- 2 teaspoons vanilla extract
- 3 cups shredded carrots (about 6 carrots)

Frosting (optional):

- 4 ounces Neufchâtel cheese
- 2 tablespoons skim milk
- 1 teaspoon vanilla extract
- 1/2 medium ripe banana, mashed

1. To prepare cake, preheat oven to 350°F; spray 12-cup Bundt pan with vegetable cooking spray; set aside.

2. In large bowl combine dry ingredients (except carrots); in medium bowl combine oil, eggs, egg whites, banana, juice concentrate, and vanilla extract; stir into dry ingredients until just blended. Fold in carrots.

3. Pour into prepared pan; bake 40–45 minutes or until toothpick inserted in center comes out clean.

4. Cool on rack 15 minutes; loosen edges with knife; remove from pan and cool completely.

5. To prepare frosting, in medium bowl combine cheese, milk, and extract; stir in banana until blended. With spatula, frost cooled cake.

Per serving:
Calories: 172   Fat: 9 g   Sodium: 177 mg   Protein: 4 g
Carbohydrate: 19 g   Cholesterol: 27 mg
Diabetic exchanges:
Starch/Bread: 1.00   Meat, Lean: 0.25   Fat: 1.50
Fruit: 0.25

🌾 Pineapple Sponge Cake

Makes 6 servings.
This is an unusual sponge cake. It's only 1 inch high and looks like a tart. After refrigeration, the bottom of this cake gets a little sticky. Place in 300°F oven for 5 minutes to dry before serving leftovers.

3   large egg whites
1/4 teaspoon cream of tartar
1   can (8 ounces) unsweetened juice-packed crushed pineapple, drained
3   tablespoons unbleached all-purpose flour
1   tablespoon dark rum
2   teaspoons vanilla extract
1/4 cup coarsely chopped macadamia nuts

1. Preheat oven to 300°F. Line an 8-inch-round baking pan with aluminum foil, folding excess foil over sides of pan; spray with nonstick cooking spray; set aside.

2. In small bowl of electric mixer, beat egg whites at high speed until frothy; add cream of tartar and beat until stiff peaks form.

3. In medium bowl combine pineapple, flour, rum, and vanilla; gently fold egg whites into mixture until combined.

4. Spoon mixture into prepared pan, smoothing top with a spatula.

5. Sprinkle nuts evenly on top; bake about 1 hour and 15 minutes until golden.

6. Gently remove cake from pan by lifting it out with the foil; cool on rack 10 minutes and carefully remove foil. Place on rack again to cool completely. Serve, preferably before refrigeration.

Per serving:
Calories: 96   Fat: 4 g   Sodium: 28 mg   Protein: 3 g
Carbohydrate: 10 g   Cholesterol: 0 mg
Diabetic exchanges:
Starch/Bread: 0.25   Meat, Lean: 0.25   Fat: 0.75
Fruit: 0.50

Pineapple Upside-Down Cake

Makes 8 servings.
Tangy and refreshing flavor in this tender cake.

- 1/4 cup reduced-calorie tub margarine, melted, divided
- 1 teaspoon ground cinnamon, divided
- 1 can (8 ounces) unsweetened juice-packed crushed pineapple, drained
- 1 1/2 cups Bisquick
- 1/4 cup evaporated skim milk
- 1/4 cup unsweetened pineapple juice concentrate
- 2 tablespoons pineapple spreadable fruit
- 1 large egg
- 2 teaspoons vanilla extract

1. Preheat oven to 350°F; drizzle 9-inch-round baking pan with 2 tablespoons margarine, tilting pan to cover; sprinkle with 1/2 teaspoon cinnamon. Spread crushed pineapple evenly into pan; set aside.

2. In large bowl of electric mixer, beat remaining ingredients at low speed 30 seconds, scraping down sides of bowl; increase to medium speed and beat 4 minutes.

3. Pour batter evenly over pineapple in pan. Bake 30–35 minutes until toothpick inserted in center comes out clean. Cool on rack 10 minutes; remove from pan by placing plate over top and inverting onto rack.

Per serving:
Calories: 201   Fat: 9 g   Sodium: 347 mg   Protein: 3 g
Carbohydrate: 27 g   Cholesterol: 27 mg
Diabetic exchanges:
Starch/Bread: 1.00   Fat: 1.75   Fruit: 0.75

Whole Wheat Carob Cake

Makes 12 servings.
Rich in carob flavor. For those who prefer chocolate, substitute cocoa powder for the carob powder. This cake freezes well.

    2   cups whole wheat pastry flour
    1   cup unbleached all-purpose flour
    1/2 cup nonfat dry milk powder
    1/2 cup carob powder
    2   teaspoons instant coffee
    2   teaspoons baking powder
    1/4 teaspoon salt
    1/2 cup unsweetened apple juice concentrate
    1/2 cup vegetable oil
    1/2 cup skim milk
    2   large eggs + 2 egg whites
    2   teaspoons chocolate extract
    1   teaspoon vanilla extract

1. Preheat oven to 350°F; spray 11-×7-inch baking pan with vegetable cooking spray; set aside.

2. In large bowl combine dry ingredients; in a 4-cup measure combine remaining ingredients. Pour liquid ingredients into dry ingredients; whisk until blended.

3. Spoon mixture into prepared pan, spreading evenly. Bake 25–30 minutes or until toothpick inserted into center comes out clean. Cool on rack 10 minutes; remove from pan and cool completely.

Per serving:
Calories: 246   Fat: 11 g   Sodium: 165 mg   Protein: 7 g
Carbohydrate: 31 g   Cholesterol: 30 mg
Diabetic exchanges:
Starch/Bread: 1.50   Meat, Med.: 0.25   Fat: 1.75
Fruit: 0.50

Brandied Bananas in Pastry Shells

Makes 4 servings.
A special treat—creamy banana filling in a flaky shell.

- 4   thawed puff pastry shells
- 3   medium-size bananas, sliced
- 1 1/2 tablespoons brandy
- 2   teaspoons fresh lemon juice
- 1/2 teaspoon ground nutmeg
- 2   tablespoons 1% low-fat milk
- Chopped pistachios to garnish, optional

1. Bake pastry shells according to package instructions; set aside.

2. Spray medium nonstick skillet with vegetable cooking spray; add bananas, brandy, lemon juice, and nutmeg. Cook over medium heat 3–5 minutes until brandy is evaporated and mixture is creamy. Remove skillet from heat; stir in milk.

3. Heap banana mixture into each shell; sprinkle with pistachios and serve immediately.

Per serving:
Calories: 296   Fat: 16 g   Sodium: 185 mg   Protein: 4 g
Carbohydrate: 37 g   Cholesterol: <1 mg
Diabetic exchanges:
Starch/Bread: 1.00   Fat: 3.00   Fruit: 1.50

3
Cookies

Gingersnaps

Makes 4 dozen cookies.
Old-fashioned flavor in this paper-thin spicy cookie.

- 7 tablespoons unsweetened apple juice concentrate
- 1/4 cup (1/2 stick) unsalted butter
- 1 1/2 cups unbleached all-purpose flour
- 1 1/2 teaspoons ground ginger
- 1/2 teaspoon ground nutmeg
- 1/4 teaspoon each baking soda and salt

1. Preheat oven to 350°F.

2. In small saucepan, over medium-high heat, combine juice concentrate and butter; stir until butter melts, remove from heat.

3. In large bowl combine remaining ingredients; pour liquid ingredients into dry, stirring until well blended.

4. On unfloured surface, roll dough as thin as possible (about 1/8-inch thick); with 1 1/2-inch-round cookie cutter, stamp out 48 cookies.

5. Bake close together on ungreased baking sheets 8–10 minutes or until crisp, dry, and lightly browned; cool on baking sheet on rack.

Per serving:
Calories: 27   Fat: 1 g   Sodium: 16 mg   Protein: <1 g
Carbohydrate: 4 g   Cholesterol: 3 mg
Diabetic exchange:
Starch/Bread: 0.33

Lemon Thins

Makes 30 cookies.
A personal favorite—bursting with lemon flavor.

- 1 1/2 cups unbleached all-purpose flour
- 1/2 teaspoon ground cinnamon
- 1/4 teaspoon each baking soda and salt
- 7 tablespoons unsweetened pineapple juice concentrate
- 1/4 cup (1/2 stick) unsalted butter, melted and cooled
- 1 1/2 teaspoons lemon extract

1. Preheat oven to 350°F.

2. In large bowl combine flour, cinnamon, baking soda, and salt; in 1-cup measure combine juice concentrate, butter, and lemon extract; pour liquid ingredients into dry, stirring until well blended.

3. On unfloured surface, shape dough into a rectangle; roll dough into a 14- × 8-inch rectangle, dusting rolling pin with flour if necessary. Cut into 2-inch squares.

4. Bake on ungreased baking sheets 10–12 minutes or until crisp and lightly browned; cool on baking sheet on rack.

Per serving:
Calories: 45   Fat: 2 g   Sodium: 25 mg   Protein: 1 g
Carbohydrate: 7 g   Cholesterol: 4 mg
Diabetic exchange:
Starch/Bread: 0.50

Oat Bran Macaroons

Makes 30 cookies.
These small mounds are chewy but light; a good way to add oat bran to your diet.

- 1/2 cup unprocessed oat bran
- 1/4 cup toasted blanched almonds
- Pinch of salt
- 1/4 cup unsweetened apple juice concentrate
- 2 tablespoons amaretto (almond-flavored liqueur)
- 2 teaspoons almond extract
- 1 teaspoon vanilla extract
- 4 large egg whites at room temperature
- 1/2 teaspoon cream of tartar

1. Preheat oven to 300°F; spray baking sheet with vegetable cooking spray; set aside.

2. In food processor fitted with steel blade, combine oat bran and almonds and salt; process until finely ground.

3. In small saucepan, over high heat, boil juice concentrate until reduced to 2 tablespoons; add amaretto and extracts; set aside.

4. In large bowl of electric mixer, beat egg whites at high speed until frothy; add cream of tartar and beat until stiff peaks form. Fold in oat bran mixture and liquid ingredients gently, until blended.

5. Drop batter by tablespoonfuls onto prepared sheet; bake 15–18 minutes or until lightly browned.

6. Turn onto rack to cool.

Per serving:
Calories: 21   Fat: 1 g   Sodium: 12 mg   Protein: 1 g
Carbohydrate: 3 g   Cholesterol: 0 mg
Diabetic exchange:
Starch/Bread: 0.25

Whole Wheat Carrot-Banana Bars

Makes 12 servings.
The natural sweetness of carrots and bananas makes a winning combination in these dense, moist bars.

- 1/2 cup unbleached all-purpose flour
- 1/2 cup whole wheat flour
- 2 teaspoons baking powder
- 1/2 teaspoon each ground ginger and cinnamon
- 4 medium carrots, cooked and mashed
- 2 medium-size ripe bananas, mashed
- 2 tablespoons unsweetened apple juice concentrate
- 1 teaspoon vanilla extract
- 1/4 cup chopped walnuts

1. Preheat oven to 350°F; spray a 9-inch-square baking pan with vegetable cooking spray; set aside.

2. In large bowl combine flours, baking powder, and spices; stir in remaining ingredients except walnuts. Spoon mixture into prepared pan; sprinkle with nuts, gently pressing into batter.

3. Bake 40–45 minutes or until toothpick inserted in center comes out clean. Cool on rack in pan 10 minutes; remove from pan and cool completely. Cut into 12 bars.

Per serving:
Calories: 87   Fat: 2 g   Sodium: 81 mg   Protein: 2 g
Carbohydrate: 16 g   Cholesterol: 0 mg
Diabetic exchanges:
Starch/Bread: 0.67   Fat: 0.25   Fruit: 0.50

Please note: The remainder of the recipes in this chapter contain no added sugar, of course, but they do derive more than 35 percent of their calories from fat. While these desserts are far healthier than most traditional recipes, you may want to save them for special occasions if fat content is your primary concern.

Blackberry Stars

Makes 20 cookies.
These light and airy puff pastry stars are delicious. A variety of cookie cutters may be used if you wish to experiment with different shapes.

    1   sheet frozen puff pastry, thawed
    1 1/2 tablespoons seedless blackberry spreadable fruit
    Ground cinnamon to garnish

1. Preheat oven to 400°F.

2. On lightly floured surface, unfold puff pastry; roll to 14- × 11-inch rectangle. With 3-inch star-cutter, stamp out 20 stars; place on baking sheet.

3. Spread each star with fruit spread and sprinkle with cinnamon. Bake 10 minutes or until puffed and crisp; remove with spatula and place on rack to cool.

Per serving:
Calories: 55   Fat: 3 g   Sodium: 58 mg   Protein: 1 g
Carbohydrate: 5 g   Cholesterol: 0 mg
Diabetic exchanges:
Fat: 0.50   Fruit: 0.50

"Cashew-Butter" Brownies

Makes 16 servings.
A cakelike brownie with nut butter instead of nuts.

- 1 cup unbleached all-purpose flour
- 1 teaspoon baking powder
- 1/4 teaspoon salt
- 1/3 cup cashew butter*
- 1 1/2 bars (3 ounces) unsweetened chocolate
- 1/2 cup unsweetened apple juice concentrate
- 2 tablespoons peach spreadable fruit
- 1 large egg, lightly beaten
- 1 teaspoon vanilla extract

1. Preheat oven to 350°F; spray 8-inch baking pan with vegetable cooking spray; set aside.

2. In small bowl combine flour, baking powder, and salt; set aside.

3. In small saucepan, over low heat, combine cashew butter and chocolate, stirring until chocolate and cashew butter are melted. Remove from heat; whisk in juice concentrate and fruit spread. Add egg and vanilla extract, whisking until mixture is smooth.

4. Stir chocolate mixture into flour mixture until just blended. Spoon into prepared pan, spreading evenly.

5. Bake about 15 minutes or until toothpick inserted in center comes out clean. Cool in pan on rack. Cut into 2-inch squares.

* Available at health food stores. There are other nut butters you may want to try.

Per serving:
Calories: 112   Fat: 6 g   Sodium: 68 mg   Protein: 3 g
Carbohydrate: 14 g   Cholesterol: 13 mg
Diabetic exchanges:
Starch/Bread: 0.50   Fat: 1.00   Fruit: 0.50

Cinnamon-Oat Squares

Makes 16.
These are very moist cookie-bars with lots of fruit flavor.

- 1 1/4 cups unbleached all-purpose flour
- 1 cup rolled oats
- 1 teaspoon baking powder
- 1 teaspoon ground cinnamon
- 1/4 teaspoon salt
- 1/2 cup (1 stick) margarine, chilled and cut into pieces
- 1/2 medium-size ripe banana, mashed
- 1/2 cup unsweetened pineapple–orange–banana juice concentrate
- 1 large egg, lightly beaten
- 1/2 teaspoon vanilla extract

1. Preheat oven to 350°F; spray 8-inch baking pan with vegetable cooking spray; set aside.

2. In large bowl combine dry ingredients; cut margarine into mixture until crumbly; add banana, juice concentrate, egg, vanilla extract, and 1/4 cup water, stirring until batter forms.

3. Spoon batter into prepared pan spreading evenly; bake 30–35 minutes or until toothpick inserted into center comes out clean. Cool on rack 10 minutes; remove from pan and turn onto rack to cool completely. Cut into squares.

Per serving:
Calories: 130   Fat: 6 g   Sodium: 133 mg   Protein: 2 g
Carbohydrate: 15 g   Cholesterol: 13 mg
Diabetic exchanges:
Starch/Bread: 1.00   Fat: 1.25

Hazelnut Biscotti

Makes about 4 dozen cookies.
These tiny, crunchy biscuitlike cookies are served with sweet wine in Italy, but they're a good match for frothy cappuccino, too.

- 1/2 cup hazelnuts (filberts)
- 13/4 cups unbleached all-purpose flour
- 3/4 teaspoon baking powder
- 1 teaspoon ground cinnamon
- 1/2 teaspoon ground nutmeg
- 1/4 teaspoon salt
- 1/4 cup unsweetened apple juice concentrate
- 3 tablespoons peach spreadable fruit
- 1 large egg + 1 egg white
- 3 tablespoons unsalted butter, melted and cooled
- 2 tablespoons cognac
- 2 teaspoons vanilla extract

1. Preheat oven to 350°F; spray baking sheet with vegetable cooking spray; set aside.

2. Spread hazelnuts in baking pan; toast in oven until skins begin to split, about 15 minutes. Carefully wrap nuts in kitchen towel and let steam 1 minute; rub to remove as much of the skin as possible.

3. In large bowl combine nuts and dry ingredients; in medium bowl whisk together remaining ingredients. Stir liquid ingredients into dry until blended.

4. Spoon dough onto prepared baking sheet and shape dough with floured hands into three 10 × 11/2-inch loaves. Bake 20–25 minutes, until loaves are firm to touch.

5. Slide loaves onto cutting board; let stand 10 minutes; with sharp knife cut diagonally into 1/2-inch-thick slices. Return loaves to baking sheet with spatula, separating and turning slices on side.

6. Bake 12–15 minutes or until lightly browned and centers are crisp. Turn onto rack to cool; store in airtight container.

Per serving:
Calories: 40   Fat: 2 g   Sodium: 21 mg   Protein: 1 g
Carbohydrate: 5 g   Cholesterol: 6 mg
Diabetic exchanges:
Fat: 0.50   Fruit: 0.50

Peanut Butter Cookies

Makes 2 1/2 dozen cookies.
Most commercial peanut butters bought in supermarkets have sugar added, so check labels. These cookies have a hint of raspberry flavor.

    6   tablespoons raspberry pourable fruit
    1   large egg at room temperature
    1   tablespoon unsalted butter, melted and cooled
    1   teaspoon vanilla extract
    1/2 cup all-natural peanut butter
    1/2 cup whole wheat flour
    1/2 cup unbleached all-purpose flour
    1/2 teaspoon baking soda
    1/4 teaspoon salt

1. Preheat oven to 375°F; spray 2 baking sheets with vegetable cooking spray; set aside.

2. In large bowl combine fruit, egg, butter, and extract; stir in peanut butter until mixture is smooth.

3. In medium bowl combine remaining ingredients; add to peanut butter mixture; stir until blended.

4. Roll small pieces of dough into 1-inch balls; place 2 inches apart on prepared sheets and flatten slightly with bottom of a glass.

5. Bake 10 minutes until firm to touch and underside is lightly browned. Turn onto rack to cool; store in airtight container.

Per serving:
Calories: 55   Fat: 3 g   Sodium: 53 mg   Protein: 2 g
Carbohydrate: 6 g   Cholesterol: 8 mg
Diabetic exchanges:
Starch/Bread: 0.33   Fat: 0.50

Peanut Butter Truffles

Makes 20 truffles.
These luscious chocolate-coated truffles are slightly sticky, but oh, so good!

- 1/2 cup all-natural peanut butter
- 1/4 cup plain bread crumbs
- 1/4 cup chopped, pitted dates
- 2 tablespoons chopped raisins
- 1 tablespoon dark rum

Chocolate coating:

- 3 tablespoons seedless raspberry pourable fruit
- 1 1/2 tablespoons cocoa powder

1. In medium bowl combine peanut butter, bread crumbs, dates, raisins, and rum until well blended. Cover and refrigerate 1 hour.

2. To prepare chocolate coating, in small bowl combine pourable fruit and cocoa until smooth. Remove peanut butter mixture from refrigerator; form into 1-inch balls. Roll each ball in coating to cover; place on plate and refrigerate at least 2 hours. When ready to serve, place in paper candy-cups.

Per serving:
Calories: 62   Fat: 3 g   Sodium: 36 mg   Protein: 2 g
Carbohydrate: 6 g   Cholesterol: trace
Diabetic exchanges:
Starch/Bread: 0.50   Fat: 0.50

Pistachio-Plum Thumbprints

Makes 24 cookies.
This cookie has lots of taste- as well as eye-appeal. Kids won't be able to keep their hands out of the cookie jar.

- 1/2 cup (1 stick) margarine at room temperature
- 1 large egg yolk
- 2 tablespoons unsweetened apple juice concentrate
- 1 teaspoon vanilla extract
- 1 cup unbleached all-purpose flour
- 1/4 teaspoon salt
- 1/4 cup finely chopped pistachio nuts
- 3 tablespoons plum spreadable fruit

1. Preheat oven to 350°F; spray baking sheet with vegetable cooking spray; set aside.

2. In food processor fitted with steel blade, combine margarine, egg yolk, juice concentrate, and vanilla extract; gradually add flour and salt, pulsing until combined.

3. Spread chopped pistachios out on wax paper. Shape dough into twenty-four 1-inch balls, roll into nuts; place about 1 inch apart on prepared sheet, pressing thumb deeply into center of each.

4. Fill each with a heaping 1/4 teaspoonful of fruit spread; bake about 12–14 minutes or until lightly browned. Turn onto rack to cool. Store in airtight container.

Per serving:
Calories: 71   Fat: 5 g   Sodium: 68 mg   Protein: 1 g
Carbohydrate: 6 g   Cholesterol: 9 mg

Diabetic exchanges:
Starch/Bread: 0.33   Fat: 1.00

Queen's Cookies

Makes 40 cookies.
A thickly coated sesame cookie great for dunking. Most local bakers are happy to sell sesame seeds by the cup or pound inexpensively. Sesame seeds are also available at health food stores.

31/4 cups unbleached all-purpose flour
1 teaspoon ground cinnamon
Pinch of salt
1/2 cup (1 stick) chilled margarine, cut into pieces
2 large eggs, separated
3/4 cup peach spreadable fruit
1/2 cup skim milk
1 cup sesame seeds

1. Preheat oven to 350°F; spray 2 baking sheets with vegetable cooking spray, set aside.

2. In large bowl sift dry ingredients; cut in margarine until mixture is crumbly.

3. In 2-cup measure combine egg yolks, fruit spread, and milk; pour into dry ingredients and mix until dough forms.

4. On lightly floured surface, knead dough 1 minute, adding a little flour if necessary. Roll into 2- × 1-inch-thick pieces. Roll each piece in egg white, then in sesame seeds to coat.

5. Place on prepared pan; bake 40–45 minutes or until browned and firm. Cool on pan on rack.

Per serving:
Calories: 96   Fat: 4 g   Sodium: 35 mg   Protein: 2 g
Carbohydrate: 12 g   Cholesterol: 11 mg
Diabetic exchanges:
Starch/Bread: 0.75   Fat: 1.00

Sesame-Oat Cookies

Makes 20 cookies.
These cookies are divine because they require no baking! Have fun and make them into different shapes—balls, logs, or discs.

- 3/4 cup rolled oats
- 1/4 cup instant nonfat dry milk
- 1/3 cup all-natural peanut butter
- 3 tablespoons unsweetened apple juice concentrate
- 1 teaspoon vanilla extract
- 1/4 cup toasted sesame seeds
- 1/2 teaspoon ground cinnamon

1. In medium bowl combine oats and dry milk; stir in peanut butter, juice concentrate, and vanilla extract.

2. Combine sesame seeds and cinnamon in a shallow dish; set aside.

3. On flat surface, shape mixture into a 10- × 1 1/2-inch log; cut into twenty 1/2-inch-wide pieces. Roll each piece into seed mixture, pressing slightly. Keep cookies covered and refrigerated.

Per serving:
Calories: 57   Fat: 3 g   Sodium: 22 mg   Protein: 2 g
Carbohydrate: 5 g   Cholesterol: <1 mg
Diabetic exchanges:
Starch/Bread: 0.33   Fat: 0.67

4

Fruit Desserts

Berries in Balsamic Vinegar

Makes 4 servings.
Balsamic vinegar is a natural grape product. It is a sweet, aged vinegar with honey overtones. This is a simple yet sophisticated dessert.

- 2 cups (1 pint) halved, hulled strawberries (use wild strawberries, if available)
- 1 cup raspberries
- 1 tablespoon balsamic vinegar
- 2 teaspoons unsweetened grape juice concentrate, optional

1. In medium bowl combine berries and vinegar; let stand at room temperature 30 minutes, stirring occasionally.

2. Taste for sweetness and flavor; add grape juice concentrate if more sweetness is desired.

Per serving:
Calories: 40   Fat: .5 g   Sodium: 1 mg   Protein: 1 g
Carbohydrate: 9 g   Cholesterol: 0 mg
Diabetic exchange:
Fruit: 0.67

Berry Crunch

Makes 4 servings.
This is an adaptation of a dessert served at the Dimmick Inn in Milford, Pa. It's elegant, yet simple and healthful.

- 1 tablespoon arrowroot
- 1/4 cup unsweetened grape juice concentrate
- 2 cups (1 pint) blueberries, rinsed and picked over
- 1/2 cup toasted fruit juice–sweetened granola*
- 2 tablespoons coarsely chopped walnuts
- 1/2 teaspoon ground cinnamon
- 1 pint (about 2 cups) strawberries, hulled and sliced

1. In a cup dissolve arrowroot in juice concentrate; pour mixture over blueberries in medium saucepan. Cook over low heat stirring frequently until thickened, about 5 minutes. Do not bring to a boil. Remove from heat and cool 10 minutes.

2. To prepare topping, in small bowl combine granola, walnuts, and cinnamon.

3. Place 1/2 cup strawberries in each of four stemmed goblets; spoon blueberry mixture evenly over strawberries; top with 2 heaping tablespoons granola mixture. Serve immediately.

* Available at health food stores.

Per serving:
Calories: 199   Fat: 4 g   Sodium: 12 mg   Protein: 3 g
Carbohydrate: 39 g   Cholesterol: 0 mg
Diabetic exchanges:
Starch/Bread: 1.00   Fat: 1.00   Fruit: 1.50

Chocolate Yogurt Cantaloupe Rings

Makes 4 servings.
The chocolate yogurt filling doubles as a summer pudding for two.

- 1 cup nonfat plain yogurt
- 1/4 cup pineapple spreadable fruit
- 2 tablespoons sour half-and-half
- 1 tablespoon cocoa powder
- 1/2 teaspoon grated orange zest
- 1/2 teaspoon vanilla extract
- 4 crosswise slices pared cantaloupe, 1/2-inch thick, seeds removed
- 1 tablespoon fresh lemon juice

1. In medium bowl combine all ingredients except cantaloupe and lemon juice until smooth. Cover and refrigerate 1 hour.

2. Place each cantaloupe ring on a dessert plate; sprinkle with lemon juice. Spoon yogurt mixture evenly into center of each ring. Serve immediately.

Per serving:
Calories: 114   Fat: 1 g   Sodium: 52 mg   Protein: 4 g
Carbohydrate: 22 g   Cholesterol: 4 mg
Diabetic exchanges:
Dairy, Skim Milk: 0.25   Fat: 0.25   Fruit: 1.25

Cranberry Grilled Grapefruit

Makes 2 servings.
*The combination of pink grapefruit and red cranberry fruit
spread is not only eye appealing but delicious.*

- 1 tablespoon cranberry sauce spreadable fruit
- 1/4 teaspoon nutmeg
- 1 medium pink grapefruit, cut in half

1. Preheat broiler.

2. In small bowl combine fruit spread and nutmeg; brush
   over grapefruit; broil 4 inches from heat 3–4 minutes
   until bubbly. Serve warm.

Per serving:
Calories: 59   Fat: .22 g   Sodium: <1 mg   Protein: 1 g
Carbohydrate: 15 g   Cholesterol: 0 mg
Diabetic exchange:
Fruit: 1.00

Creamy Baked Bananas

Makes 4 servings.
Lots of zesty sweet flavor in this soft-textured banana dish. For aficionados of fresh bananas,* here's a variation.

- 1 1/2   tablespoons unsweetened pineapple–orange–banana juice concentrate
- 1   tablespoon Neufchâtel cheese, at room temperature
- 2   teaspoons fresh lemon juice
- 2   teaspoons margarine, at room temperature
- 1/2   teaspoon ground allspice
- 3   medium-size ripe bananas
- 2   tablespoons light cream, optional

1. Preheat oven to 375°F.

2. In small food processor combine all ingredients except bananas; pulse until blended.

3. Cut bananas in half, crosswise then lengthwise; place in 9-inch baking dish, cut-side down; pour cheese mixture evenly over bananas.

4. Bake about 15 minutes or until hot and bubbly. Cool to room temperature; drizzle with cream.

---

* *Variation:* Place fresh bananas on dessert dishes. In small saucepan, over medium heat, cook sauce 3–5 minutes until boiling, stirring frequently. Pour over bananas.

Per serving:
Calories: 117   Fat: 3 g   Sodium: 38 mg   Protein: 1 g
Carbohydrate: 23 g   Cholesterol: 3 mg
Diabetic exchanges:
Fat: 0.50   Fruit: 1.50

Fruit with Peach Custard Sauce

Makes 4 servings.
Ribbons of this light and lovely sauce add the perfect amount of sweetness and contrast to these summer fruits.

- 1 cup halved, hulled strawberries
- 1 cup raspberries
- 2 kiwi fruit, pared and sliced 1/4-inch thick

Custard:

- 1/2 cup 1% low-fat milk
- 2 large egg whites
- 2 tablespoons peach spreadable fruit

1. Arrange fruit in individual dessert dishes; set aside.

2. To prepare custard, pour milk into top of double boiler. Cook over boiling water for 5 minutes. Do not let the milk boil.

3. In small bowl whisk egg whites until frothy; gradually stir in 1/4 cup hot milk into whites. Whisk mixture into remaining hot milk, stirring constantly. Cook about 3 minutes longer or until sauce thickens, stirring constantly. Remove mixture from heat and whisk in fruit spread. Drizzle over fruit; serve at room temperature (you may refrigerate it up to 30 minutes).

Per serving:
Calories: 92   Fat: 1 g   Sodium: 45 mg   Protein: 4 g
Carbohydrate: 19 g   Cholesterol: 1 mg
Diabetic exchanges:
Meat, Lean: 0.50   Fruit: 1.25

Grapefruit in Warm Blackberry Sauce

Makes 4 servings.
Frozen blackberries (thawed) work very well in this dessert.

- 1 medium grapefruit, peeled, segmented, and coarsely chopped
- 1 cup blackberries
- 1 tablespoon blackberry spreadable fruit

1. Divide grapefruit evenly among 4 dessert dishes; set aside.

2. In small saucepan, over low heat, combine blackberries, fruit spread, and 1 tablespoon water; cook about 5 minutes, stirring occasionally until fruit spread dissolves and blackberries become syrupy.

3. Spoon blackberry mixture evenly over grapefruit.

Per serving:
Calories: 48 Fat: <1 g Sodium: 0 mg Protein: 1 g
Carbohydrate: 12 g Cholesterol: 0 mg
Diabetic exchange:
Fruit: 0.75

Grilled Summer Figs

Makes 4 servings.
The simplicity and lusciousness of this dessert is noteworthy.

12 whole fresh figs*
1/4 cup marsala or port wine, optional

1. Spray grill rack with vegetable cooking spray; prepare grill following manufacturer's instructions.

2. Skewer figs; place over low setting of gas grill or burned-out but still warm coals; grill 6 minutes or just until figs begin to swell and skin dries out.

3. Remove from skewers; cut in half lengthwise. Place 6 fig halves on individual serving plates; drizzle with wine.

Per serving:
Calories: 113   Fat: 1 g   Sodium: 2 mg   Protein: 1 g
Carbohydrate: 29 g   Cholesterol: 0 mg
Diabetic exchange:
Fruit: 2.00

* Fresh figs may be purchased at better greengrocers in late summer and early fall.

Grilled Tropical Fruit with Coconut "Cream"

Makes 4 servings.

Carambola, a waxy yellow star-shaped fruit, is now produced in Florida. It usually appears at the market in August. If it's unavailable, double up on kiwifruit.

- 2 kiwifruits, pared and sliced into 1/2-inch-thick rounds
- 2 starfruit (carambola) sliced into 1/2-inch-thick rounds
- 1/2 small pineapple, pared and cut crosswise into 4 equal rounds and quartered
- 1 medium-size banana, peeled and halved lengthwise and crosswise
- 1/4 cup plain low-fat yogurt
- 3/4 teaspoon coconut flavoring
- 2 tablespoons unsweetened toasted coconut

1. Spray grill rack with vegetable cooking spray; prepare grill, following manufacturer's instructions.

2. Place fruits over low setting of gas grill or burned-out but still warm coals; grill fruits 3 minutes on each side.

3. In small bowl combine yogurt and coconut flavoring; spoon over fruit and sprinkle with coconut.

Per serving:
Calories: 128   Fat: 3 g   Sodium: 15 mg   Protein: 2 g
Carbohydrate: 27 g   Cholesterol: 1 mg
Diabetic exchanges:
Fat: 0.50   Fruit: 1.75

Lemon-Ginger Pear Cobbler

Makes 6 servings.
A super-quick dessert to assemble—outstanding lemon flavor.

- 2 cans (16-ounce) drained unsweetened juice-packed pear halves, reserving 1/4 cup juice
- 2 cups Bisquick
- 1/2 teaspoon each ground ginger and cinnamon
- 1/2 cup skim milk
- 1 1/2 teaspoons vanilla extract
- 1 teaspoon lemon extract

1. Preheat oven to 425°F; place pears and reserved juice in an 8-inch-square baking pan; set aside.

2. In medium bowl combine Bisquick and spices; stir in remaining ingredients until just blended.

3. Drop batter by spoonfuls onto pears; bake 35–45 minutes or until browned and toothpick inserted into center comes out clean. Cool on rack 5 minutes.

Per serving:
Calories: 245   Fat: 5 g   Sodium: 483 mg   Protein: 4 g
Carbohydrate: 46 g   Cholesterol: <1 g
Diabetic exchanges:
Starch/Bread: 1.00   Fat: 1.00   Fruit: 2.00

Macadamia Nectarines (Microwave)

Makes 4 servings.
The combination of fresh nectarines and juice cooked in a microwave produces a light and luscious syrup.

- 4 medium (about 1 pound) nectarines
- 2 tablespoons unsweetened pineapple juice

Topping:

- 1/2 cup plain nonfat yogurt
- 2 tablespoons coarsely chopped macadamia nuts
- 2 tablespoons unsweetened pineapple juice
- 1 teaspoon vanilla extract
- 1/4 teaspoon ground allspice

1. Place 1 nectarine in each of 4 custard cups; drizzle evenly with juice.

2. Cover cups with vented plastic wrap; microwave on High for 5 minutes, rotating cups once until nectarines are soft; cool 10 minutes.

3. In small bowl combine remaining ingredients; spoon evenly over nectarines.

Per serving:
Calories: 109   Fat: 4 g   Sodium: 22 mg   Protein: 3 g
Carbohydrate: 17 g   Cholesterol: <1 g
Diabetic exchanges:
Dairy, Skim Milk: 0.13   Fat: 0.75   Fruit: 1.00

Melon Balls in Citrus Syrup

Makes 6 servings.
Light and refreshing melon sampler.

- 1/2 cup orange juice
- 3 tablespoons orange marmalade spreadable fruit
- 1 tablespoon unsweetened pineapple juice concentrate
- 1 teaspoon fresh lemon juice
- 4 cups melon balls (cantaloupe, honeydew, watermelon)

1. In small saucepan combine orange juice, fruit spread, juice concentrate, and lemon juice; cook over high heat about 3 minutes, stirring constantly until marmalade dissolves and mixture is reduced slightly. Remove from heat; cool 5 minutes.

2. In medium bowl combine melon balls and orange juice syrup; toss to coat. Cover and refrigerate 2 hours, stirring occasionally.

Per serving:
Calories: 73   Fat: <1 g   Sodium: 8 mg   Protein: 1 g
Carbohydrate: 18 g   Cholesterol: 0 mg
Diabetic exchange:
Fruit: 1.25

Minted Peaches

Makes 4 servings.
This light, refreshing dessert may be served year-round. If fresh mint is unavailable, substitute 1/4 teaspoon mint extract.

- 1/4 cup light cream
- 2 teaspoons finely chopped fresh mint
- 8 unsweetened juice-packed drained canned peach halves
- 11/2 tablespoons finely chopped pistachio nuts
- Mint sprigs to garnish, optional

1. In small bowl combine cream and mint; cover and refrigerate 30 minutes.

2. Place peaches on serving platter; drizzle with cream mixture; sprinkle with pistachios.

Per serving:
Calories: 114   Fat: 4 g   Sodium: 12 mg   Protein: 2 g
Carbohydrate: 19 g   Cholesterol: 10 mg

Diabetic exchanges:
Fat: 1.00   Fruit: 1.25

Mulled Oranges

Makes 4 servings.
This is a lovely winter dessert full of the flavor of the season. For a dramatic presentation, stud a small orange with cloves; place in center of serving platter and arrange orange slices around it.

- 3/4 cup orange juice
- 1/4 cup orange-flavored liqueur
- 8 whole cloves
- 1 3-inch cinnamon stick
- 1/4 teaspoon ground nutmeg
- 4 small navel oranges (about 3/4 pound), peeled and separated into segments

1. In small saucepan, over high heat, combine all ingredients except oranges. Bring to a boil and reduce heat to medium; simmer about 15 minutes, stirring occasionally until liquid is slightly reduced.

2. Place orange segments in a bowl; toss with orange syrup. Cover and refrigerate overnight. Remove cloves and cinnamon stick before serving.

Per serving:
Calories: 91   Fat: <1 g   Sodium: 1 mg   Protein: 1 g
Carbohydrate: 17 g   Cholesterol: 0 mg
Diabetic exchange:
Fruit: 1.50

Raspberries Romanoff

Makes 4 servings.
A lighter version of a classic dessert.

- 2 cups fresh raspberries
- 2 tablespoons unsweetened grape juice concentrate
- 2 tablespoons orange-flavored liqueur
- 2 cups nonfat plain yogurt
- 1/4 cup light cream, optional

1. In medium bowl combine raspberries, juice concentrate, and liqueur; cover and refrigerate 1 hour, stirring occasionally.

2. Spoon 1/2 cup yogurt into each of 4 stemmed goblets; divide raspberry mixture evenly over yogurt; drizzle each with 1 tablespoon cream.

Per serving:
Calories: 134   Fat: <1 g   Sodium: 87 mg   Protein: 7 g
Carbohydrate: 23 g   Cholesterol: 2 mg
Diabetic exchanges:
Dairy, Skim Milk: 0.50   Fruit: 1.00

Roasted Pears

Makes 4 servings.
Roasting fruit allows natural juices to become thick and syrupy.

- 4 Bosc pears, whole (about 2 pounds)
- 1/2 cup dry red wine
- 1/4 cup unsweetened grape juice concentrate
- 2 teaspoons cornstarch, dissolved in 2 tablespoons water
- 1/4 cup light cream, optional

1. Preheat oven to 450°F.

2. In medium saucepan, over medium heat, combine pears, wine, juice concentrate, and 1/4 cup water. Cover and cook 10 minutes.

3. Remove pears with slotted spoon to cutting board; cool. Reserve wine mixture.

4. Cut pears in half and remove core, leaving stem. Spray an 11-inch ceramic quiche dish or shallow baking pan with vegetable cooking spray; place pears cut-side down in dish. Bake 15 minutes.

5. In medium saucepan bring wine mixture to a boil over medium heat; add cornstarch mixture and boil 1 minute, stirring constantly. Remove from heat.

6. Pour 1 tablespoon cream into each of 4 shallow soup dishes; place 2 pear halves cut-side down in cream; spoon wine sauce evenly over pears.

Per serving:
Calories: 191   Fat: 1 g   Sodium: 3 mg   Protein: 1 g
Carbohydrate: 43 g   Cholesterol: 0 mg
Diabetic exchanges:
Fat: 0.25   Fruit: 3.00

Sherried Fruit

Makes 4 servings.
Just minutes to make this appetizing dessert.

- 1/3 cup sweet sherry
- 1 large orange, peeled and thinly sliced crosswise into 16 rounds
- 1 cup red seedless grapes, halved

1. In small saucepan, over medium heat, bring sherry to a boil. Remove from heat and cool.

2. Remove seeds from sliced oranges; arrange in a shallow 8-inch bowl in circles to cover dish. Add grapes forming an outer ring around oranges. Pour sherry over fruit evenly. Cover and refrigerate 2 hours.

Per serving:
Calories: 68   Fat: <1 g   Sodium: 2 mg   Protein: <1 g
Carbohydrate: 12 g   Cholesterol: 0 mg
Diabetic exchanges:
Fat: 0.50   Fruit: 0.75

The Ultimate Baked Apple

Makes 4 servings.
These glazed apples are equally delicious served warm or cold.

- 4 Rome Beauty or Golden Delicious apples (2¼ pounds)
- ¼ cup chopped walnuts
- ½ teaspoon grated lemon zest
- ½ teaspoon ground cinnamon
- ¼ cup unsweetened apple juice concentrate
- 1 tablespoon arrowroot dissolved in 2 tablespoons water

Light cream or plain yogurt to garnish, optional

1. Preheat oven to 375°F.

2. Core apples and pare top half; place in 8-inch-square baking dish and pour 1 cup water into dish.

3. In small bowl combine walnuts, lemon zest, cinnamon; stuff each apple with mixture, reserving remainder.

4. Pour apple juice concentrate over apples evenly; sprinkle with remaining nut mixture.

5. Bake 30–40 minutes or until tender when pierced with fork; baste apples with liquid several times during baking.

6. Place apples on serving dish.

7. Pour remaining basting juices into small saucepan; stir in arrowroot mixture. Cook over medium heat until thickened, stirring constantly, but do not bring to a boil.

8. Spoon glaze over apples and serve.

Per serving:
Calories: 216   Fat: 5 g   Sodium: 5 mg   Protein: 2 g
Carbohydrate: 45 g   Cholesterol: 0 mg
Diabetic exchanges:
Fat: 1.00   Fruit: 3.00

Please note: The final recipe in this chapter contains no added sugar, of course, but it does derive more than 35 percent of its calories from fat. While it is far healthier than most traditional recipes, you may want to save it for special occasions if fat content is your primary concern.

Chocolate-Coated Fruit Party Platter

Makes 12 servings of 3 pieces.
This thick, delicious chocolate coating is bittersweet in flavor.
For a mellower taste add a little Grand Marnier or Triple Sec.
Recipe may be halved.

- 4 ounces unsweetened chocolate squares
- 1 tablespoon unsalted butter
- 1/2 cup unsweetened apple juice concentrate
- 1 teaspoon vanilla extract
- 4 cups fresh fruit (whole strawberries, bananas, navel orange slices, kiwis, etc.)

1. Spray baking sheet with vegetable cooking spray; set aside.

2. In top of double boiler, over simmering water, melt chocolate and butter, stirring occasionally; remove from heat and cool slightly. Whisk in juice concentrate a little at a time until chocolate is smooth; add vanilla extract. If mixture is too thick, add a little more concentrate until it thins out.

3. Dip ends of fruit into chocolate mix, twirling to coat lower half of each piece of fruit; let excess drip back into pan until all chocolate is used.

4. Place fruit on prepared baking sheets; place in freezer 10 minutes to set chocolate. Refrigerate until ready to serve.

Per serving:
Calories: 108   Fat: 6 g   Sodium: 4 mg   Protein: 2 g
Carbohydrate: 15 g   Cholesterol: 3 mg
Diabetic exchanges:
Fat: 1.25   Fruit: 1.00

5

Pies, Tarts, Turnovers, and Crepes

Blueberry Crepes

Makes 10 crepes.
A versatile dessert: substitute any preferred flavor fruit spread or fresh fruit topping.

Crepes:

1 cup skim milk
1/2 cup whole wheat pastry flour
1/2 cup unbleached all-purpose flour
1 large egg + 2 egg whites
1 tablespoon vegetable oil
1 teaspoon vanilla extract
1/8 teaspoon baking powder
Pinch of salt

Filling:

1 container (15 ounces) part-skim ricotta cheese
2 tablespoons wild blueberry spreadable fruit
1 teaspoon vanilla extract
1/2 teaspoon grated lemon zest
1/2 teaspoon ground cinnamon

Topping:

2 cups fresh or frozen blueberries
2 tablespoons unsweetened grape juice concentrate

1. To prepare crepes, in medium bowl whisk together all ingredients, cover, and refrigerate 1 hour.

2. To prepare filling, in food processor fitted with steel blade, combine all ingredients; pulse until well blended.

3. Spray a crepe pan or 7- or 8-inch nonstick sauté pan with vegetable cooking spray. Heat over medium-high heat until a drop of water jumps across pan.

4. For each crepe, pour a scant 1/4 cup of the batter into center of pan; immediately rotate pan until batter covers bottom. Cook 1–2 minutes, until underside is light brown and dry; run spatula around edges and lift out. Turn and cook 1 minute longer. Place crepe on foil.

5. After each crepe is lifted from pan, remove pan from heat and spray with nonstick cooking spray. Repeat with remaining batter.

6. In small saucepan combine blueberries and juice concentrate; cook 10 minutes over medium-high heat, stirring frequently.

7. Spoon about 3 tablespoons of the filling in center of each crepe. Fold sides of crepe over filling, overlapping the edges. Invert onto serving dish, folded side down. Spoon sauce evenly over each.

Per serving:
Calories: 169   Fat: 6 g   Sodium: 104 mg   Protein: 9 g
Carbohydrate: 21 g   Cholesterol: 35 mg
Diabetic exchanges:
Starch/Bread: 0.50   Meat, Lean: 1.00   Fat: 0.50
Fruit: 1.00

Blueberry Pie

Makes 8 servings.
This versatile pie can be made with frozen blueberries.

Pastry:

- 2 cups unbleached all-purpose flour
- 3/4 teaspoon salt
- 1/4 cup chilled margarine, cut into pieces
- 3 tablespoons chilled reduced-calorie margarine
- 5–6 tablespoons ice water

Filling:

- 5 cups (2 pints) blueberries washed and picked over
- 1 tablespoon fresh lemon juice
- 1/2 cup blueberry pourable fruit
- 1/4 cup cornstarch
- 1 teaspoon ground cinnamon
- 1/8 teaspoon salt

1. To prepare pastry, in large bowl or food processor fitted with steel blade combine flour and salt; cut in margarine or pulse until mixture resembles coarse crumbs. Add water 1 tablespoon at a time until dough forms. Press dough into ball and flatten; wrap in plastic wrap and refrigerate 30 minutes.

2. Preheat oven to 425°F.

3. To prepare filling, place blueberries in large bowl; sprinkle with lemon juice; stir in pourable fruit until blended. On wax paper combine cornstarch, cinnamon, and salt; sprinkle over blueberries and toss well; set aside.

4. Cut dough in half; on lightly floured surface, roll one half into an 11-inch circle; fold in half and place in 9-inch pie plate; unfold and fill with blueberry mixture. Roll remaining dough into a 10-inch circle; carefully place over filling. Press edges to seal; crimp with fingers. Make 6 slits near center.

5. Bake 50–60 minutes until lightly browned. Cool on rack 30 minutes.

Per serving:
Calories: 287   Fat: 9 g   Sodium: 368 mg   Protein: 4 g
Carbohydrate: 50 g   Cholesterol: 0 mg
Diabetic exchanges:
Starch/Bread: 1.25   Fat: 1.75   Fruit: 1.75

Buckwheat Dessert Blini

Makes 14 blini (7 servings).
*A dessert version of Russian blini (tiny pancakes) that are tradi-
tionally served with sour cream and caviar.*

Blini:

- 1/2 cup skim milk
- 1 teaspoon yeast
- 2 large eggs, separated, at room temperature
- 3/4 cup buckwheat flour
- 1 tablespoon vegetable oil
- 2 teaspoons peach spreadable fruit
- 1 teaspoon vanilla extract
- 1/4 teaspoon salt

Topping:

- 1/3 cup sour half-and-half
- 2 tablespoons nonfat plain yogurt
- 1/8 teaspoon black walnut extract
- 1/3 cup seedless blackberry spreadable fruit

1. To prepare blini, in small saucepan scald milk over high
   heat; cool to lukewarm and stir in yeast; set aside.

2. In large bowl of electric mixer, beat egg yolks at high
   speed until thick and creamy, about 5 minutes. Whisk in
   milk mixture and remaining ingredients, except egg
   whites. Cover with plastic wrap; let rise in warm draft-
   free place until doubled in size, about 1 1/2 hours.

3. In small bowl of electric mixer, beat egg whites at high
   speed until stiff peaks form. Fold into batter until
   blended.

4. Spray small nonstick skillet with vegetable cooking spray; heat over medium high heat until a drop of water jumps across skillet.

5. Drop 1 heaping tablespoonful of batter into hot skillet; cook 1 minute on each side, turning with spatula. Repeat with remaining batter, coating pan with vegetable cooking spray each time.

6. In small bowl combine sour cream alternative, yogurt, and black walnut extract; spread thickly on each blin. Drop a dollop of fruit spread in center and serve.

Per serving:
Calories: 145   Fat: 5 g   Sodium: 112 mg   Protein: 5 g
Carbohydrate: 20 g   Cholesterol: 65 mg
Diabetic exchanges:
Starch/Bread: 1.00   Fat: 1.00   Fruit: 0.33

Fresh Peach Pie

Makes 8 servings.
Juicy and delectable—a highlight during summer months.

Pastry:

- 1 3/4 cups unbleached all-purpose flour
- 1 teaspoon grated lemon zest
- 1/4 teaspoon salt
- 1/2 cup reduced-calorie tub margarine
- 2 tablespoons unsweetened apple juice concentrate

Filling:

- 8 medium peaches (about 2 pounds)
- 2 tablespoons fresh lemon juice
- 1 teaspoon vanilla extract
- 1/2 cup peach spreadable fruit
- 2 tablespoons cornstarch
- 1/2 teaspoon ground cinnamon
- 1/8 teaspoon salt

1. To prepare pastry, in large bowl or food processor fitted with steel blade, combine flour, zest, and salt; add margarine and juice concentrate, pulsing until dough forms. Press dough into ball and flatten; wrap in plastic wrap and refrigerate 30 minutes.

2. Preheat oven to 350°F.

3. To prepare filling, in large pot of boiling water blanch peaches 1 minute; remove with slotted spoon; cool under running water. Peel, halve, pit, and cut into 1/4-inch slices. Place in large bowl; sprinkle with lemon juice and vanilla extract and toss well. Stir in peach spread until combined. On wax paper, combine cornstarch, cinnamon, and salt; add to peach mixture and toss until well coated.

4. Cut dough in half; on lightly floured surface, roll one half into an 11-inch circle. Fold in half and place in 9-inch pie plate; unfold and fill with peach mixture. Roll remaining dough into a 10-inch circle; carefully place over filling. Press edge to seal; crimp with fingers. Make 6 slits near center.

5. Bake 50–60 minutes until lightly browned. Cool on rack 30 minutes.

Per serving:
Calories: 247   Fat: 6 g   Sodium: 214 mg   Protein: 3 g
Carbohydrate: 45 g   Cholesterol: 0 mg
Diabetic exchanges:
Starch/Bread: 1.50   Fat: 1.25   Fruit: 1.50

Fruit-Bread Tart

Makes 8 servings.
An unusual and luscious Italian dessert from the Tuscany region of Italy. A great play on texture—crispy pears, creamy custard, and juicy grapes.

- 6   slices day-old firm-textured white bread, quartered diagonally
- 1½ cups skim milk
- 1/3 cup raisins
- 3   large eggs
- 1/4 cup yellow cornmeal
- 2   teaspoons vanilla extract
- 1/2 teaspoon grated lemon zest
- 1   cup seedless red grapes
- 1   Anjou pear (about 8 ounces), pared, cored, and chopped
- 2   teaspoons chopped fresh rosemary
- 2   teaspoons olive oil

1. In medium bowl combine milk and raisins; let stand 10 minutes.

2. Preheat oven to 350°F; spray 9-inch cake pan with vegetable cooking spray; place bread in pan to cover bottom (bread will overlap).

3. To milk mixture, add eggs, cornmeal, vanilla, and lemon zest; pour over bread, pressing bread down with spoon to cover. Add grapes and pear; sprinkle with rosemary; drizzle with oil.

4. Bake 40–45 minutes or until knife inserted in center comes out clean.

Per serving:
Calories: 173   Fat: 4 g   Sodium: 157 mg   Protein: 6 g
Carbohydrate: 28 g   Cholesterol: 81 mg
Diabetic exchanges:
Starch/Bread: 1.00   Meat, Med.: 0.50   Fat: 0.25
Fruit: 0.75

Fruit Empanadas

Makes 38.
These tiny turnovers may be filled with a variety of dried fruits, jams, or drained, unsweetened canned fruits.

Pastry:

- 1/3   cup chopped dates
- 1   cup unbleached all-purpose flour
- 1/2   cup whole wheat flour
- 2   tablespoons pumpkin seeds
- 1   teaspoon baking powder
- 1/2   teaspoon salt
- 6   tablespoons reduced-calorie tub margarine, chilled
- 4–5   tablespoons ice water

Filling:

- 1   cup chopped dried mixed fruit
- 1/2   cup chopped dates
- 1/4   teaspoon ground cloves

Glaze:

- 1   large egg white, lightly beaten

1. To prepare pastry, in small saucepan combine dates with 1/3 cup water. Cook over low heat until mushy, about 10 minutes. Place in food processor fitted with steel blade; add dry ingredients; process 20 seconds. Add margarine; pulse until crumbly. Add water, 1 tablespoon at a time, and pulse until ball forms. Flatten dough into a dish; refrigerate overnight.

2. Preheat oven to 375°F; spray 2 baking sheets with vegetable cooking spray; set aside.

3. To prepare filling, in small saucepan combine dried fruits and cloves with 1 cup water. Cook over low heat, covered, until mushy and syrupy, stirring occasionally, about 15 minutes. Cool and puree in food processor.

4. Cut dough in half. On lightly floured surface, roll dough to 1/8-inch thickness. With 3-inch biscuit cutter, stamp out 19 circles. Repeat with remaining dough. Fill with 2 teaspoons filling; pinch ends to close. Brush with egg white.

5. Bake 20–25 minutes until golden; turn onto rack to cool.

Per serving:
Calories: 47   Fat: 1 g   Sodium: 60 mg   Protein: 1 g
Carbohydrate: 9 g   Cholesterol: 0 mg
Diabetic exchanges:
Starch/Bread: 0.25   Fat: 0.25   Fruit: 0.33

Fruit-Meringue Tarts

Makes 6 tarts.
Fluffy meringue mounds in easy crust. Make with your favorite flavor fruit spread.

Pastry:

    1   cup whole wheat pastry flour
    1/2 cup unbleached all-purpose flour
    1/4 teaspoon ground nutmeg
    Pinch of salt
    3   tablespoons vegetable oil
    2–4 tablespoons ice water

Filling:

    3   large egg whites at room temperature
    1/8 teaspoon cream of tartar
    1/3 cup spreadable fruit

1. To prepare pastry, in medium bowl combine flours, nutmeg, and salt; stir in oil then water, 1 tablespoon at a time until dough forms; knead 5 times. Flatten dough into disc; wrap in plastic wrap, and refrigerate 30 minutes.

2. Preheat oven to 375°F; spray six 4-inch tart pans with vegetable cooking spray; set aside.

3. To prepare filling, in large bowl of electric mixer, beat egg whites at high speed until frothy; add cream of tartar and beat 20 seconds. Add fruit spread and continue beating at high speed until stiff peaks form; set aside.

4. On lightly floured surface, divide dough into 6 equal pieces. Press 1 piece into each prepared pan, gently pushing up sides to cover. Prick bottom with a fork several times. Place on baking sheet.

5. Bake shells 10 minutes; cool on rack 10 minutes. Raise oven temperature to 425°F.

6. Return tart pans to baking sheet; mound fruit meringue evenly in pans. Bake 5–7 minutes or until well browned. Remove from baking sheet and cool on rack.

Per serving:
Calories: 211   Fat: 7 g   Sodium: 51 mg   Protein: 6 g
Carbohydrate: 32 g   Cholesterol: 0 mg

Diabetic exchanges:
Starch/Bread: 1.25   Fat: 1.50   Fruit: 1.00

Granny Smith Pie

Makes 8 servings.
Deliciously tart apples are mounded high in a flaky crust. For sweeter palates, use Golden Delicious apples.

Pastry:

- 2 cups unbleached all-purpose flour
- 3/4 teaspoon salt
- 1/2 teaspoon ground cinnamon
- 1/3 cup reduced-calorie tub margarine
- 2 tablespoons vegetable oil
- 5–6 tablespoons ice water

Filling:

- 2 tablespoons unsweetened apple juice concentrate
- 2 tablespoons apple butter
- 6 cups 1/4-inch-thick pared apple slices (about 2 pounds)
- 2 tablespoons cornstarch
- 2 teaspoons ground cinnamon
- 1/2 teaspoon grated lemon zest

1. To prepare pastry, in large bowl or food processor fitted with steel blade, combine flour, salt, and cinnamon; cut in margarine or pulse until mixture resembles coarse crumbs. Pour oil and water into flour mixture and mix well until dough forms. Press dough into ball and flatten; wrap in plastic wrap and refrigerate 30 minutes.

2. Preheat oven to 425°F.

3. To prepare filling, in large bowl combine apple juice concentrate and apple butter; add apples; toss until blended. On wax paper combine cornstarch, cinnamon, and lemon zest; sprinkle over apple mixture and toss well.

4. Cut dough in half; press one half into 9-inch pie plate, gently pushing and spreading dough across bottom and up sides of plate to fit with a 1-inch overlap; fill with apple mixture. Place remaining dough between 2 sheets of wax paper; roll into a 10-inch circle. Remove top piece of wax paper; gently lift dough with paper and invert onto apple mixture; remove wax paper. Press edges to seal; crimp with fingers. Make 6 slits near center.

5. Bake 50–60 minutes until lightly browned. Cool on rack 30 minutes.

Per serving:
Calories: 257   Fat: 8 g   Sodium: 281 mg   Protein: 3 g
Carbohydrate: 44 g   Cholesterol: 0 mg
Diabetic exchanges:
Starch/Bread: 1.50   Fat: 1.50   Fruit: 1.50

Plantain Fritters

Makes 8 servings.
Plantains used in this dessert should be fully ripe—black and yielding slightly to the touch.

    1/2 cup unbleached all-purpose flour
    1/4 teaspoon ground allspice
    1/4 teaspoon salt
    1/2 cup skim milk
    2 tablespoons pineapple spreadable fruit
    1 tablespoon vegetable oil
    1 large egg white, stiffly beaten
    4 ripe plantains (about 4 cups), cut on diagonal 1/2-inch thick*
    Oil to depth of 1/2 inch in skillet (about 2 cups)**

1. In large bowl combine flour, allspice, and salt; in 2-cup measure combine milk, fruit spread, and vegetable oil. Pour liquid ingredients into dry ingredients; whisk to combine. Cover and refrigerate 30 minutes.

2. Fold egg white into flour mixture; add plantain slices, toss to coat.

3. In 12-inch skillet heat oil over medium-high heat, 7–10 minutes or until a drop of water jumps across skillet. Add plantain slices; cook about 1 minute on each side until deep golden brown; turn with slotted spatula and cook about 30 seconds. (If oil gets too hot, plantains will cook faster.) Adjust heat.

* Ripe but firm bananas may be substituted and are naturally sweeter.
** Note: 11/2 cups remaining oil may be strained, refrigerated, and reused for deep frying.

Per serving:
Calories: 226   Fat: 8 g   Sodium: 86 mg   Protein: 3 g
Carbohydrate: 38 g   Cholesterol: <1 g

Diabetic exchanges:
Starch/Bread: 0.50   Fat: 1.67   Fruit: 2.00

Quick Cherry Blintzes

Makes 4 servings.
You may never make crepes for blintzes again, once you've used egg roll wrappers!

Topping:

1 cup fresh or frozen dark pitted cherries
1/2 cup unsweetened mountain cherry juice
1 teaspoon arrowroot

Filling:

1 cup low-fat creamed or small curd cottage cheese
1/4 cup low-fat yogurt
1/3 cup peach spreadable fruit
4 egg roll wrappers
3 tablespoons vegetable oil

1. To prepare topping, in small saucepan combine cherries and juice; cook over medium heat 5 minutes, stirring occasionally. Stir in arrowroot; cook 3–5 minutes until slightly thickened. Do not boil. Keep sauce warm.

2. In small bowl whisk together cheese, yogurt, and fruit spread until blended.

3. To prepare blintzes, spoon heaping 1/4 cup filling into center of each egg roll wrapper. Fold 2 opposite ends to center over filling; fold each remaining end over center to form a 41/2-× 3-inch rectangle.

4. In medium skillet heat oil over medium heat until a drop of water jumps across skillet; add 2 blintzes. Cook 3 minutes on each side or until browned; drain on paper towels. Repeat with remaining blintzes. Serve with warm sauce.

Per serving:
Calories: 322   Fat: 12 g   Sodium: 249 mg   Protein: 12 g
Carbohydrate: 43 g   Cholesterol: 3 mg
Diabetic exchanges:
Starch/Bread: 1.00   Meat, Lean: 1.00   Fat: 1.75
Fruit: 1.75

Please note: The remainder of the recipes in this chapter contain no added sugar, of course, but they do derive more than 35 percent of their calories from fat. While these desserts are far healthier than most traditional recipes, you may want to save them for special occasions if fat content is your primary concern.

Apple Strudel

Makes 8 servings.
Apple strudel is the "queen" of strudels. These thin pastry layers may be filled with a variety of fruits.

- 3 Golden Delicious apples (about 1 pound), pared, cored, and chopped
- 1 tablespoon reduced-calorie tub margarine
- 2 teaspoons fresh lemon juice
- 1/2 teaspoon ground cinnamon
- 1 sheet thawed puff pastry
- 3 tablespoons chopped walnuts
- 1 large egg white, lightly beaten with 1 tablespoon water

1. In medium saucepan combine apples, 1/2 cup water, margarine, lemon juice, and cinnamon; cook over medium heat about 20 minutes, stirring frequently until apples are tender and liquid has evaporated; cool 15 minutes.

2. On lightly floured surface, roll pastry to a 14- × 10-inch rectangle; place on ungreased baking sheet.

3. Spoon apple mixture lengthwise down center third of pastry; sprinkle with walnuts; brush edges with egg white mixture. Fold pastry on left side over filling, then pastry on right side to form strudel. Pinch edges to seal; turn pastry over so seam side is down. Brush with remaining egg white mixture; refrigerate 30 minutes.

4. Preheat oven to 425°F; using a sharp knife, make 3 slits in top of pastry without cutting through pastry. Bake 30 minutes or until puffed and golden. Cool on rack 30 minutes.

Per serving:
Calories: 185   Fat: 11 g   Sodium: 166 mg   Protein: 2 g
Carbohydrate: 19 g   Cholesterol: 0 mg
Diabetic exchanges:
Starch/Bread: 0.67   Fat: 2.25   Fruit: 0.50

Apple Turnovers

Makes 12.
The marketing of frozen puff pastry is a boon to every baker. It makes these light and delicious turnovers a snap to prepare.

- 2 medium apples (about 2 cups), pared and shredded
- 2 teaspoons cornstarch
- 1 teaspoon fresh lemon juice
- 1/2 teaspoon ground cinnamon
- 1 sheet thawed puff pastry
- 1/4 cup apple butter
- 1 large egg white, lightly beaten

1. Preheat oven to 350°F; spray baking sheet with vegetable cooking spray; set aside.

2. In medium bowl combine apples, cornstarch, lemon juice, and cinnamon; set aside.

3. On lightly floured surface, roll pastry to a 12- × 16-inch rectangle; using a ruler as guide, cut twelve 4-inch squares. Brush each square liberally with apple butter. Spoon a heaping tablespoon of apple mixture in center of each square; fold in half diagonally. Seal by pressing fork tines around edges. Brush each turnover with egg white; place on prepared sheet.

4. Bake about 25 minutes or until brown and crispy; turn onto rack to cool.

Per serving:
Calories: 112   Fat: 6 g   Sodium: 101 mg   Protein: 1 g
Carbohydrate: 13 g   Cholesterol: 0 mg

Diabetic exchanges:
Starch/Bread: 0.50   Fat: 1.00   Fruit: 0.50

Kiwi Tart

Makes 8 servings.
A fabulous citrus-flavored filling in a crisp shell makes this summer tart a menu must.

Pastry:

- 1/4 cup (1/2 stick) margarine at room temperature
- 1 tablespoon pineapple spreadable fruit
- 1 large egg white
- 3/4 cup unbleached all-purpose flour
- Pinch of salt

Filling:

- 1 tablespoon unbleached all-purpose flour
- 1 package unflavored gelatin
- 1/8 teaspoon salt
- 1/2 cup half-and-half
- 1/2 cup skim milk
- 1/2 cup unsweetened pineapple juice concentrate
- 1 tablespoon dark rum
- 1 tablespoon lime juice
- 1 teaspoon vanilla extract
- 3 ripe kiwifruit

1. In medium bowl of electric mixer, cream margarine and fruit spread at medium speed until fluffy; add egg white; beat at high speed until smooth.

2. At low speed gradually blend in flour and salt until dough forms. Flatten dough into disc. Wrap in plastic wrap; refrigerate 30 minutes.

3. Preheat oven to 300°F; spray an 8- or 9-inch tart pan (with removable rim) with vegetable cooking spray.

4. Turn dough into prepared pan; press evenly over bottom and up sides. Bake about 40 minutes or until golden. Cool in pan on rack 10 minutes; remove rim.

5. To prepare filling, in medium saucepan combine flour, gelatin, and salt. In 2-cup measure, combine half-and-half, skim milk, juice concentrate, rum, and lime juice. Pour into saucepan; cook over medium heat, whisking frequently until mixture thickens and comes to a gentle boil, about 10 minutes. Remove from heat; add vanilla extract.

6. Pour mixture into medium bowl set in a pan with ice and water; let stand, stirring occasionally until mixture begins to set, about 10 minutes. Pour mixture into prepared shell, spreading evenly; cover lightly with foil; refrigerate 30 minutes.

7. Pare and thinly slice kiwifruit; place in slightly overlapping circles on filling. Cover and refrigerate at least 1 hour before serving.

Per serving:
Calories: 189   Fat: 8 g   Sodium: 142 mg   Protein: 4 g
Carbohydrate: 25 g   Cholesterol: 6 mg
Diabetic exchanges:
Starch/Bread: 0.50   Dairy, Skim Milk: 0.25   Fat: 1.50
Fruit: 1.00

6

Puddings, Custards, Mousses, Soufflés, and Compotes

Apple-Currant Compote (Microwave)

Makes 4 servings.
A lovely combination of fresh and dried fruit with a minimum of fuss.

- 4 small (about 1 1/4 pounds) Golden Delicious apples, cored and cut into 8 slices each
- 1/4 cup dried currants
- 2 tablespoons sliced almonds
- 1/2 teaspoon ground cinnamon
- 1/4 cup apricot pourable fruit
- 1 tablespoon margarine

1. Place apples, currants, and almonds in a 9-inch microwave-safe dish; sprinkle with cinnamon.

2. Spoon pourable fruit over apple mixture; dot with margarine.

3. Cover with vented plastic wrap; microwave on High for 8 minutes, rotating dish after 4 minutes.

Per serving:
Calories: 182   Fat: 5 g   Sodium: 47 mg   Protein: 1 g
Carbohydrate: 36 g   Cholesterol: 0 mg
Diabetic exchanges:
Fat: 1.00   Fruit: 2.50

Brandied Peach Sauce

Makes 1 1/2 cups, or six 1/4 cup servings.
This topping is perfect on plain cake, yogurt, and fresh fruit medleys. May be served warm or cold.

- 1 (16-ounce) can unsweetened juice-packed sliced peaches, drained, reserving 3 tablespoons juice
- 1 teaspoon brandy extract
- 1 teaspoon vanilla extract

Combine peaches, reserved juice, brandy extract, and vanilla extract in blender container; puree until smooth. May be frozen.

Per serving:
Calories: 38   Fat: trace   Sodium: 3 mg   Protein: <1 g
Carbohydrate: 9 g   Cholesterol: 0 mg
Diabetic exchange:
Fruit: 0.67

Cantaloupe Chiffon

Makes 4 servings.
Use only very ripe, sweet cantaloupe for this light dessert.

- 1 package gelatin
- 1 medium-size ripe cantaloupe (about 2 cups)
- 3 tablespoons low-fat sour cream alternative
- 1 tablespoon lemon juice
- 1/4 teaspoon ground cinnamon
- Julienne of lemon peel to garnish

1. In small saucepan sprinkle gelatin over 1/4 cup cold water; let stand 1 minute. Stir over low heat until gelatin is dissolved.

2. In food processor fitted with steel blade, combine remaining ingredients; gradually add gelatin mixture; process until blended.

3. Divide mixture evenly among 4 dessert bowls; refrigerate until firm (about 1 hour). Garnish with lemon peel.

Per serving:
Calories: 50   Fat: 1 g   Sodium: 15 mg   Protein: 3 g
Carbohydrate: 7 g   Cholesterol: 0 mg
Diabetic exchanges:
Fat: 0.25   Fruit: 0.50

Caramel Custard

Makes 12 servings.
Rich caramel flavor in this tasty custard. Slices up beautifully.

- 2   cans (12 ounces) evaporated skimmed milk
- 2   large eggs + 2 egg whites
- 1/2   cup peach spreadable fruit
- 1   tablespoon arrowroot
- 11/2 teaspoons vanilla extract
- 1/2   teaspoon caramel extract
- 1/8   teaspoon salt

1. Preheat oven to 350°F; spray 81/2- × 41/2-inch loaf pan with vegetable cooking spray; set aside.

2. In blender combine all ingredients until smooth. Pour into prepared pan; put into 11- × 7-inch baking pan; place on oven rack. Pour boiling water into larger pan to come halfway up sides of loaf pan.

3. Bake 1 hour or until knife inserted in center comes out clean. Remove pan from water; cool on rack. Refrigerate 2 hours before serving. Run knife around rim of pan; invert onto plate to remove.

Per serving:
Calories: 98   Fat: 1 g   Sodium: 116 mg   Protein: 6 g
Carbohydrate: 15 g   Cholesterol: 38 mg
Diabetic exchanges:
Dairy, Skim Milk: 0.50   Fruit: 0.75

Carob Soufflé

Makes 8 servings.
Carob, also known as St. John's bread, comes from the pods of the tropical carob tree. It's often used as a chocolate substitute, but only vaguely resembles chocolate in flavor.

    4   large eggs, separated, at room temperature
    1/2 teaspoon cream of tartar
    3/4 cup instant nonfat dry milk
    1/2 cup carob powder
    1/2 cup part-skim ricotta cheese
    3   tablespoons unsweetened apple juice concentrate
    1   teaspoon vanilla extract

1. Preheat oven to 350°F; spray 6-cup soufflé dish with vegetable cooking spray; set aside.

2. In large bowl with electric mixer at high speed, beat egg whites until frothy; add cream of tartar and beat until stiff peaks form; set aside.

3. In medium bowl whisk yolks and remaining ingredients until smooth; fold half of mixture into whites until combined; repeat with remaining half.

4. Spoon mixture into prepared dish; bake 30 minutes. Serve immediately.

Per serving:
Calories: 106   Fat: 4 g   Sodium: 94 mg   Protein: 7 g
Carbohydrate: 10 g   · Cholesterol: 112 mg

Diabetic exchanges:
Dairy, Skim Milk: 0.50   Meat, Med.: 0.50   Fat: 0.25
Fruit: 0.25

Cherry Pudding (Microwave)

Makes 8 servings.
A sweet pudding that takes less than 15 minutes to make.

- 1/4 cup cornstarch
- 1 1/2 tablespoons unbleached all-purpose flour
- 1/4 teaspoon salt
- 2 cups skim milk
- 1 large egg
- 1/2 cup black cherry spreadable fruit
- 1/4 cup chopped dried red tart cherries
- 1 tablespoon margarine
- 1 teaspoon vanilla extract

1. In 1 1/2-quart casserole combine cornstarch, flour, and salt; whisk in milk until smooth. Microwave on High for 5 minutes or until slightly thickened, beating well with whisk every 2 minutes.

2. In small bowl combine egg, spreadable fruit, and cherries; whisk in 1/2 cup hot milk mixture, whisking constantly. Slowly add egg mix to milk mixture.

3. Microwave on High for 1 minute or until pudding thickens, stirring once. Stir in margarine and vanilla extract until margarine melts.

4. Refrigerate 2 hours or until chilled. Whisk before serving.

Per serving:
Calories: 119   Fat: 2 g   Sodium: 124 mg   Protein: 3 g
Carbohydrate: 21 g   Cholesterol: 28 mg

Diabetic exchanges:
Dairy, Skim Milk: 0.25   Fat: 0.50   Fruit: 1.25

Clementine Soufflé

Makes 6 servings.
These tiny, tasty soufflés may be served warm, at room tempera-
ture, or cold. They never collapse!

- 2 large eggs, separated, at room temperature
- 1/4 teaspoon cream of tartar
- 1/2 cup skim milk
- 1/3 cup orange juice
- 2 teaspoons vanilla extract
- 3 tablespoons unbleached all-purpose flour
- 3 clementine oranges, peeled and separated into segments

1. Preheat oven to 325°F; spray six 4-ounce custard cups with vegetable cooking spray; set aside.

2. In small bowl of electric mixer, beat egg whites at high speed until frothy; add cream of tartar and beat until stiff peaks form; set aside.

3. In large bowl of electric mixer, beat egg yolks at high speed 5 minutes until thick and lemon-colored; on low speed beat in milk, orange juice, and vanilla extract. Whisk in flour, then oranges; carefully fold in egg whites a little at a time until blended.

4. Spoon mixture into prepared cups; place in 11- × 7-inch baking pan; place on oven rack. Pour boiling water into baking pan to cover halfway up sides of cups.

5. Bake 30 minutes or until browned and firm; remove cups from water and place on rack.

Per serving:
Calories: 77   Fat: 2 g   Sodium: 32 mg   Protein: 4 g
Carbohydrate: 11 g   Cholesterol: 71 mg

Diabetic exchanges:
Meat, Lean: 0.50   Fruit: 0.75

Cranberry-Banana Compote

Makes 4 servings.
A delicious and colorful compote; high in vitamin C and potassium.

- 1/2 cup orange juice
- 2 tablespoons cranberry sauce spreadable fruit
- 1/2 cup fresh cranberries, picked over
- 3 medium-size ripe bananas, cut on diagonal 1/2-inch thick
- 1 tablespoon fresh lemon juice

. In small saucepan combine juice and fruit spread; whisk over medium heat 2–3 minutes, stirring frequently until fruit spread dissolves. Add cranberries; cook 10 minutes, stirring occasionally. Let cool 15 minutes.

. In medium bowl toss bananas with lemon juice; place on serving dish; divide cranberry mixture evenly over bananas and serve.

Per serving:
Calories: 121   Fat: <1 g   Sodium: 1 mg   Protein: 1 g
Carbohydrate: 31 g   Cholesterol: 0 mg
Diabetic exchange:
Fruit: 2.00

Gingered Pumpkin Flan

Makes 12 servings.
A dense custard, cut into wedges. Looks and tastes like a crustless pumpkin pie.

- 1 1/2 cups mashed, cooked pumpkin (canned or fresh)
- 1 can (12 ounces) evaporated skimmed milk
- 1/3 cup apricot spreadable fruit
- 2 large eggs + 2 egg whites
- 2 teaspoons vanilla extract
- 3/4 teaspoon ground ginger
- 1/4 teaspoon ground cinnamon
- Pinch of salt
- 1/2 cup half-and-half, optional

1. Preheat oven to 350°F; spray 9-inch-round baking pan with vegetable cooking spray; set aside.

2. In large bowl combine all ingredients, whisking until blended. Pour into prepared pan; put into large baking pan; place on oven rack. Pour boiling water into larger pan to come halfway up the sides of 9-inch pan.

3. Bake 40–45 minutes or until knife inserted in center comes out clean. Remove pan from water; cool on rack. Refrigerate 2 hours before serving. Run knife around rim of pan; cut into 12 wedges; drizzle with half-and-half.

Per serving:
Calories: 70   Fat: 1 g   Sodium: 65 mg   Protein: 4 g
Carbohydrate: 11 g   Cholesterol: 37 mg
Diabetic exchanges:
Vegetables: 1.00   Meat, Med.: 0.25   Fruit: 0.50

Mango-Rum Pudding

Makes 4 servings.
A delightfully light pudding.

- 2 mangoes, peeled and pitted
- 1/2 cup evaporated skimmed milk
- 3 tablespoons unsweetened pineapple–orange–banana juice concentrate
- 1/2 teaspoon rum extract

Toasted unsweetened coconut to garnish, optional

In food processor fitted with steel blade, combine all ingredients until smooth; spoon into dessert dishes; refrigerate 2 hours. Sprinkle with coconut before serving.

Per serving:
Calories: 117   Fat: <1 g   Sodium: 40 mg   Protein: 3 g
Carbohydrate: 26 g   Cholesterol: 1 mg
Diabetic exchanges:
Dairy, Skim Milk: 0.25   Fruit: 1.50

Mocha Mousse Parfait

Makes 6 servings.
Delightfully light and frothy coffee-flavored pudding with a thick layer of bananas.

- 1 cup hot water
- 1 tablespoon instant coffee powder
- 1/2 teaspoon vanilla extract
- 1/3 cup apricot pourable fruit
- 1 cup instant nonfat dry milk
- 1/4 teaspoon ground cinnamon
- 3 medium-size ripe bananas, sliced 1/4-inch thick
- 6 whole strawberries, to garnish

1. In small bowl of electric mixer, combine water, coffee powder, and vanilla; whisk in pourable fruit until blended. Cover and refrigerate 1 hour.

2. Add dry milk powder and cinnamon to bowl; with mixer running at low speed, combine for 20 seconds. Beat mixture until thick and fluffy at high speed, about 10 minutes. Cover and refrigerate 30 minutes.

3. Fill parfait or 12-ounce stemmed glasses halfway with mocha "cream"; add a layer of bananas. Fill to top with mocha "cream." Garnish with strawberries; cover and refrigerate 2 hours, but not longer than 4 hours, before serving.

Per serving:
Calories: 127   Fat: <1 g   Sodium: 74 mg   Protein: 5 g
Carbohydrate: 28 g   Cholesterol: 2 mg
Diabetic exchanges:
Dairy, Skim Milk: 0.50   Fruit: 1.50

Noodle Kugel

Makes 12 servings.
*An Eastern European pudding often served with poppy seeds during the Christmas season—*dee-licious!

   12 ounces no-egg-yolk noodles
   1 cup part-skim ricotta
   3/4 cup nonfat plain yogurt
   3/4 cup golden raisins
   1/2 cup low-fat sour cream alternative
   2 large eggs, lightly beaten
   1/4 cup unsweetened apple juice concentrate
   2 teaspoons vanilla extract
   1 teaspoon ground cinnamon
   1/8 teaspoon salt
   Ground cinnamon to garnish

1. Preheat oven to 350°F; spray 13-×9-inch baking pan with vegetable cooking spray; set aside.

2. In large pot of boiling water cook noodles according to package directions; drain and spoon into prepared pan.

3. In large bowl combine remaining ingredients; pour evenly over noodles, slightly tossing with a fork; sprinkle with cinnamon. Bake about 30 minutes or until lightly browned.

Per serving:
Calories: 201   Fat: 4 g   Sodium: 89 mg   Protein: 9 g
Carbohydrate: 33 g   Cholesterol: 42 mg
Diabetic exchanges:
Starch/Bread: 1.25   Dairy, Skim Milk: 0.50   Fat: 0.75
Fruit: 0.50

Peaches and Port Bread Pudding

Makes 8 servings.
This lovely summer pudding is rich in flavor and low in fat.

- 13/4 cups skim milk
- 11/2 tablespoons unsalted butter
- 6 slices stale firm-textured bread, cut into 1-inch pieces*
- 2 medium ripe peaches (about 10 ounces), peeled, pitted, and chopped
- 2 tablespoons toasted pignoli nuts
- 1/3 cup port wine
- 1/3 cup peach spreadable fruit
- 2 large eggs + 2 egg whites
- 11/2 teaspoons vanilla extract
- 1/4 teaspoon nutmeg
- 1/8 teaspoon salt

1. Preheat oven to 350°F; spray 9-×5-inch loaf pan with vegetable cooking spray; set aside.

2. In medium saucepan, over medium heat, combine milk and butter; cook until film forms on top. Remove from heat and cool until lukewarm.

3. In prepared pan alternately layer bread cubes (plus crumbs from the cut bread), peaches, and pignoli nuts; set aside.

4. In large bowl whisk port, fruit spread, eggs and whites, vanilla, nutmeg, and salt until well combined.

5. Pour into prepared pan over bread layers; bake 1 hour and 15 minutes or until a deep golden color.

* To make fresh bread stale, place in 250°F oven 10 minutes.

6. Cool in pan on rack. To remove, run knife around rim and invert onto serving plate.

Per serving:
Calories: 188   Fat: 5 g   Sodium: 201 mg   Protein: 7 g
Carbohydrate: 25 g   Cholesterol: 61 mg
Diabetic exchanges:
Starch/Bread: 0.75   Dairy, Skim Milk: 0.25
Meat, Med.: 0.25   Fat: 1.00   Fruit: 0.67

Pear and Mango Clafouti

Makes 10 servings.
A peasant pudding from France. This version, using summer Bartlett pears, lends crispness and contrast to tender and soft mangoes.

    2   tablespoons unsalted margarine
    3   medium Bartlett pears (about 1½ pounds), cored,
        pared, and coarsely chopped
    1   large mango (about 1½ pounds), peeled, pitted, and
        coarsely chopped
    2   tablespoons chopped pistachio nuts
    ¾   cup unsweetened apple juice
    2   large eggs + 2 egg whites
    ¼   cup unsweetened apple butter
    1   teaspoon vanilla extract
    ⅓   cup unbleached all-purpose flour
    ⅓   cup whole wheat pastry flour
    ½   teaspoon baking powder
    ¼   teaspoon ground mace
    ⅛   teaspoon salt

1. Preheat oven to 400°F; spray an 11- × 7½-inch baking pan with vegetable cooking spray; set aside.

2. In 12-inch nonstick skillet, melt margarine over medium-high heat; add pears and cook until just tender, about 10 minutes, stirring occasionally. Spoon pears and mango into prepared pan; sprinkle with nuts and set aside.

3. In medium bowl whisk juice, eggs, and egg whites, apple butter, and vanilla until smooth; in small bowl combine remaining ingredients. Sift dry ingredients into liquid; stir until blended.

4. Pour batter over fruit in pan; bake about 35 minutes until puffy and golden or until toothpick inserted in center comes out clean. Place pan on rack to cook 10–15 minutes. Serve warm or at room temperature.

Per serving:
Calories: 167   Fat: 5 g   Sodium: 75 mg   Protein: 4 g
Carbohydrate: 30 g   Cholesterol: 43 mg
Diabetic exchanges:
Starch/Bread: 0.50   Meat, Med.: 0.25   Fat: 0.75
Fruit: 1.50

Persimmon Mousse

Makes 6 servings.
Persimmons, a bright orange, late fall/winter fruit, can be enjoyed year-round. Pare and spoon flesh into a sealable freezer bag. Defrost and use in sauces, puddings, and sherbets.

- 1   package unflavored gelatin
- 1/2 cup water
- 2   persimmons (about 2 cups), pared and chopped
- 2/3 cup instant nonfat dry milk
- 1/3 cup peach spreadable fruit
- 6   ice cubes
- 1/4 cup light cream, optional

1. In small saucepan sprinkle gelatin over water; let stand 1 minute. Bring to boil over medium heat, stirring until gelatin dissolves.

2. In blender combine gelatin mixture, persimmons, milk powder, and spreadable fruit; process until smooth. Add ice cubes one at a time, until blended.

3. Pour into 1-quart bowl; cover and refrigerate 2 hours. Serve drizzled with light cream.

Per serving:
Calories: 79   Fat: trace   Sodium: 43 mg   Protein: 4 g
Carbohydrate: 16 g   Cholesterol: 1 mg
Diabetic exchanges:
Dairy, Skim Milk: 0.33   Fruit: 0.75

Ricotta Soufflé

Makes 8 servings.
Fabulous soufflé. Tastes like amaretti *cookies. When cooled and refrigerated, it will collapse a little but becomes a light cheese-cake.*

1 container (15 ounce) part-skim ricotta cheese
1/2 cup plain bread crumbs
1/3 cup peach spreadable fruit
2 large eggs, separated + 3 egg whites, at room temperature
1 tablespoon finely chopped sliced almonds
1 teaspoon each almond and vanilla extract
1/2 teaspoon cream of tartar

1. Preheat oven to 375°F; spray 6-cup soufflé dish with vegetable cooking spray; set aside.

2. In large bowl whisk ricotta, bread crumbs, fruit spread, egg yolks, almonds, and extracts until well blended; set aside.

3. In small bowl of electric mixer, beat egg whites at high speed until frothy; add cream of tartar and beat until stiff peaks form. Gently fold 1/3 whites into ricotta mix until thoroughly blended; repeat procedure with remaining whites. Spoon into prepared dish, spreading top evenly.

4. Bake 35–40 minutes until puffed and golden. Serve immediately as a soufflé.

Per serving:
Calories: 159   Fat: 6 g   Sodium: 149 mg   Protein: 10 g
Carbohydrate: 15 g   Cholesterol: 70 mg

Diabetic exchanges:
Starch/Bread: 0.50   Meat, Lean: 1.25   Fat: 0.50
Fruit: 0.75

Semolina Pudding

Makes 6 servings.
This is an adaptation of a dessert served in India called sonji halwa.

    2   cups unsweetened white grape juice
1/3 cup dark raisins
1/4 cup reduced-calorie tub margarine
    1   cup semolina (farina)
1/4 teaspoon each ground cardamom and mace
1/4 cup 1% low-fat milk
    2   tablespoons light cream

1. Combine grape juice and raisins; set aside.

2. In 12-inch nonstick skillet, over medium heat, melt margarine. Stir in semolina; cook 10 minutes, stirring frequently, until golden.

3. Pour juice–raisin mixture into skillet in a steady stream, stirring rapidly with a whisk to prevent lumping; bring to a boil. Reduce heat and simmer 5–7 minutes, stirring frequently, until liquid is absorbed. Stir in spices.

4. Remove from heat; stir in milk and cream. Serve warm or at room temperature.*

* *Variation:* Spray an 8-inch-square baking pan with vegetable cooking spray; pour in pudding; cover and refrigerate overnight. To serve, invert onto cutting board and cut into squares. Top with warm pourable fruit.

Per serving:
Calories: 233   Fat: 5 g   Sodium: 89 mg   Protein: 4 g
Carbohydrate: 43 g   Cholesterol: 4 mg
Diabetic exchanges:
Starch/Bread: 1.50   Fat: 1.00   Fruit: 1.33

Tangy Peach Pudding

Makes 4 servings
This zesty fruit blend has a tofu base yielding a nondairy dessert.

- 1 teaspoon unflavored gelatin
- 1/3 cup unsweetened pineapple–orange–banana juice concentrate
- 1 teaspoon almond extract
- 1 cup (about 10 ounces) drained tofu
- 1/2 medium-size ripe banana
- 3 tablespoons peach spreadable fruit
- Pinch of salt
- 1 can (16 ounces) unsweetened, juice-packed sliced peaches, drained and chopped

1. In small saucepan sprinkle gelatin over juice concentrate; let stand 1 minute. Cook over low heat until gelatin dissolves, stirring occasionally. Add almond extract.

2. In food processor fitted with steel blade, combine remaining ingredients except peaches; process until smooth. Add gelatin mixture; pulse until combined. Fold in peaches.

3. Divide mixture evenly into 4 dessert bowls; cover and refrigerate at least 1 hour before serving.

Per serving:
Calories: 193   Fat: 3 g   Sodium: 45 mg   Protein: 8 g
Carbohydrate: 35 g   Cholesterol: 0 mg
Diabetic exchanges:
Meat, Med.: 0.75   Fruit: 2.25

Warm Cider Compote

Makes 6 servings.
A luscious winter compote of stewed dried fruits to complement the season.

 1 1/2 cups apple cider
 4 lemon peel strips (2 inches long)
 1 tablespoon fresh lemon juice
 1/2 cup coarsely chopped mixed dried fruits
 1/4 cup raisins
 1/4 cup halved dried apricots
 1/4 cup halved dried pitted dates
 8 dried Calimyrna figs stemmed and halved
 1/4 cup dried red tart cherries
 6 tablespoons half-and-half

1. In medium saucepan combine cider, lemon zest, and juice; bring to boil over high heat.

2. Add fruit; cover and reduce heat to low; simmer 12–15 minutes, stirring occasionally until fruit is soft.

3. Spoon into 6 dishes; drizzle with half-and-half.

Per serving:
Calories: 210 Fat: 2 g Sodium: 15 mg Protein: 2 g
Carbohydrate: 50 g Cholesterol: 6 mg
Diabetic exchanges:
Fat: 0.50 Fruit: 3.25

Winter Bread Pudding

Makes 8 servings.
This delicious pudding has a slightly crusty top and a soft, sweet center with lots of maple flavor.

- 2 1/2 cups 1% low-fat milk
- 2 large eggs + 2 egg whites
- 1/2 cup unsweetened apple juice concentrate
- 1/4 cup chopped pitted dates
- 2 tablespoons currants
- 1 teaspoon maple extract
- 1 teaspoon vanilla extract
- 1/4 teaspoon ground cinnamon
- 4 cups (about 1/2 loaf) French bread cut into 1 1/2-inch cubes

1. Preheat oven to 350°F. Spray 8-× 8-inch baking pan with vegetable cooking spray; set aside.

2. In large bowl whisk together all ingredients except bread.

3. Place bread in prepared pan; stir milk mixture and pour evenly over bread; press bread down with spoon to cover.

4. Bake, covered, 30 minutes; uncover and bake 30 minutes longer. Let stand 10 minutes before serving.

Per serving:
Calories: 155   Fat: 3 g   Sodium: 165 mg   Protein: 7 g
Carbohydrate: 26 g   Cholesterol: 57 mg
Diabetic exchanges:
Starch/Bread: 0.50   Meat, Med.: 0.50   Fruit: 1.25

Please note: The final recipe in this chapter derives more than 35 percent of its calories from fat. If fat content is your primary concern, you may want to save this recipe for special occasions.

Crème Fraîche

Makes 3/4 cup or 12 servings.
Has a pleasant sour taste, richer than sour cream with much less fat than heavy cream. Serve with fresh or grilled fruits or as a garnish on sorbets.

   1/2 cup half-and-half
   1 tablespoon lowfat buttermilk
   1/4 cup plain nonfat yogurt

1. In glass jar combine first two ingredients; cover lightly with towel and let stand at room temperature overnight.

2. Stir in yogurt; refrigerate covered up to 1 week.

Per serving:
Calories: 16   Fat: 1 g   Sodium: 9 mg   Protein: 1 g
Carbohydrate: 1 g   Cholesterol: 4 mg
Diabetic exchange:
Fat: 0.25

7

Tea Cakes and Quick Breads

Applesauce Coffee Cake

Makes 12 servings.
This raisin-rich coffee cake is spicy.

- 1 cup unbleached all-purpose flour
- 1 cup whole wheat flour
- 1/2 cup golden raisins
- 3 tablespoons finely chopped pecans
- 1 1/2 teaspoons baking powder
- 1 teaspoon baking soda
- 1/2 teaspoon each ground nutmeg and cloves
- 1/8 teaspoon ground ginger
- 1/8 teaspoon salt
- 1 1/4 cups unsweetened applesauce
- 3 tablespoons unsweetened apple juice concentrate
- 2 tablespoons vegetable oil
- 1 large egg, lightly beaten

1. Preheat oven to 325°F; spray 11-×7-inch baking pan with vegetable cooking spray; set aside.

2. In large bowl, combine dry ingredients. In 2-cup measure combine applesauce, juice concentrate, oil, and egg; add to flour mixture; stir until just blended.

3. Pour batter into prepared pan; bake about 20 minutes or until toothpick inserted in center comes out clean. Cool on rack 10 minutes; remove from pan and cool completely.

Per serving:
Calories: 148   Fat: 4 g   Sodium: 153 mg   Protein: 3 g
Carbohydrate: 25 g   Cholesterol: 18 mg
Diabetic exchanges:
Starch/Bread: 1.00   Fat: 0.75   Fruit: 0.67

Banana-Prune Bread

Makes 1 loaf or 12 servings.
This firm and moist bread is perfect for children's lunchboxes
and there are no crumbs. Two thin slices of this bread make the
perfect peanut butter and fruit spread sandwich.

- 2 medium ripe bananas
- 2 large eggs, lightly beaten
- 1/3 cup unsweetened prune juice with pulp
- 1 teaspoon vanilla extract
- 1 1/2 cups unbleached all-purpose flour
- 1 cup whole wheat flour
- 1/2 cup chopped pitted prunes
- 1 teaspoon baking soda
- 1/2 teaspoon ground cinnamon
- 1/4 teaspoon salt

1. Preheat oven to 350°F; spray 9- × 5-inch loaf pan with vegetable cooking spray. Set aside.

2. In large bowl mash bananas; stir in eggs, prune juice, and vanilla.

3. In large bowl combine remaining ingredients; stir into banana mixture until just blended.

4. Spoon into prepared pan; bake 50–60 minutes or until toothpick inserted in center comes out clean.

5. Cool on rack 10 minutes; remove from pan and cool completely.

Per serving:
Calories: 144   Fat: 1 g   Sodium: 126 mg   Protein: 4 g
Carbohydrate: 29 g   Cholesterol: 35 mg
Diabetic exchanges:
Starch/Bread: 1.33   Fat: 0.25   Fruit: 0.50

Irish Soda Bread

Makes 1 loaf or 16 servings.
Lots of caraway flavor and plump raisins in this delicious cake-like bread.

- 4 cups self-rising flour
- 1 cup dark raisins
- 2 tablespoons caraway seeds
- 1 1/2 cups 1% low-fat milk
- 1/4 cup unsweetened apple juice concentrate

1. Preheat oven to 375°F; spray 9-inch baking pan with vegetable cooking spray; set aside.

2. In large bowl combine flour, raisins, and caraway seeds; gradually add milk and juice concentrate to form a runny batter.

3. Pour into prepared pan, spreading evenly; bake 30–35 minutes or until toothpick inserted in center comes out clean and top is lightly browned.

4. Cool on rack 10 minutes; remove from pan. May be served warm or cooled. Freezes well.

Per serving:
Calories: 158   Fat: 1 g   Sodium: 411 mg   Protein: 4 g
Carbohydrate: 34 g   Cholesterol: 1 mg
Diabetic exchanges:
Starch/Bread: 1.50   Fruit: 0.75

Quick Holiday Fruitcake

Makes 1 loaf or 12 servings.
The flavor of rum permeates this rich, dense, sweet fruitcake. A slice goes a long way during the indulgent holiday festivities.

- 1 1/2 cups unbleached flour
- 1/2 cup whole wheat flour
- 1 teaspoon salt
- 1 teaspoon each ground cinnamon and cloves
- 1/2 cup unsweetened grape juice concentrate
- 1/3 cup margarine, melted and cooled
- 2 large eggs
- 2 teaspoons rum extract
- 1 teaspoon vanilla extract
- 1/4 cup raisins
- 1/4 cup chopped dates
- 1/4 cup chopped mixed dried fruit
- 1/4 cup coarsely chopped walnuts

1. Preheat oven to 300°F; line 8 1/2- × 4 1/2-inch loaf pan with foil; set aside.

2. In large bowl combine dry ingredients. In medium bowl combine juice concentrate and 1/3 cup water, margarine, eggs, and extracts. Add liquid ingredients to dry; stir until just blended. Fold in dried fruits and walnuts.

3. Spoon into prepared pan; bake 1 hour and 15 minutes or until toothpick inserted in center comes out clean. Cover with foil if top browns too quickly. Cool on rack in pan; carefully remove foil before serving.

Per serving:
Calories: 206   Fat: 8 g   Sodium: 256 mg   Protein: 4 g
Carbohydrate: 30 g   Cholesterol: 35 mg
Diabetic exchanges:
Starch/Bread: 1.00   Fat: 1.50   Fruit: 1.00

Tea Scones

Makes 12.
Scones are the Scottish cousin of the American biscuit. Denser and slightly sweet, they are served with preserves and slightly soured cream, such as Crème Fraîche.

- 1 1/2 cups unbleached all-purpose flour
- 2 teaspoons baking powder
- 1/4 teaspoon salt
- 1/4 cup (1/2 stick) unsalted butter, chilled and cut into pieces
- 1/3 cup golden raisins
- 1 large egg, lightly beaten
- 1/3 cup unsweetened apple juice concentrate

1. Preheat oven to 425°F; spray baking sheet with vegetable cooking spray; set aside.

2. In large bowl combine flour, baking powder, and salt; with a pastry blender or 2 knives, cut in butter until mixture is crumbly.

3. Stir in remaining ingredients until dough forms; turn onto lightly floured surface; knead gently about 12 times.

4. Roll dough into 1/2-inch thickness; with a 2 1/4-inch floured biscuit cutter, cut into 12 rounds.

5. Bake 10–12 minutes or until lightly browned and firm to touch.

Per serving:
Calories: 123   Fat: 5 g   Sodium: 125 mg   Protein: 2 g
Carbohydrate: 18 g   Cholesterol: 28 mg
Diabetic exchanges:
Starch/Bread: 0.75   Fat: 1.00   Fruit: 0.50

Please note: **The remainder of the recipes in this chapter contain no added sugar, of course, but they do derive more than 35 percent of their calories from fat. While these desserts are far healthier than most traditional recipes, you may want to save them for special occasions if fat content is your primary concern.**

Apricot Coffee Cake

Makes 10 servings.
This is a moist, dense cake with plenty of eye appeal. Also good with plums.

- 1/3 cup margarine at room temperature
- 1/3 cup unsweetened apple juice concentrate
- 1 large egg + 2 egg whites at room temperature
- 2 teaspoons vanilla extract
- 1 cup unbleached all-purpose flour
- 1 teaspoon baking powder
- 1/4 teaspoon salt
- 1 teaspoon ground allspice, divided
- 5 small apricots (about 1/2 pound), halved and pitted

1. Preheat oven to 350°F; spray 8-inch springform pan with vegetable cooking spray; set aside.

2. In food processor fitted with steel blade, combine margarine, juice concentrate, egg, egg whites, and vanilla extract.

3. In medium bowl combine flour, baking powder, salt, and 1/2 teaspoon allspice; gradually add to margarine mixture, pulsing until blended.

4. Pour batter into prepared pan; arrange apricots, skin-side down, on top, gently pressing into batter. Sprinkle with remaining allspice.

5. Bake 25–30 minutes or until toothpick inserted in center comes out clean. Cool on rack 5 minutes; remove from pan and cool completely.

Per serving:
Calories: 140   Fat: 7 g   Sodium: 187 mg   Protein: 3 g
Carbohydrate: 16 g   Cholesterol: 21 mg
Diabetic exchanges:
Starch/Bread: 0.75   Fat: 1.38   Fruit: 0.25

Fruit-and-Nut Crescents

Makes 8 servings.
This sweet and satisfying treat is perfect for an afternoon coffee break. A single serving can be made in a toaster oven.

- 1   8-ounce package refrigerated crescent rolls
- 1/4   cup apricot pourable fruit
- 2   tablespoons coarsely chopped sliced almonds
- 1/4   teaspoon ground cinnamon

1. Preheat oven to 375°F.

2. Unroll dough; place separated triangles on baking sheet. Brush each triangle with fruit; sprinkle evenly with nuts and cinnamon. Roll loosely from shorter side of triangle to opposite point. Brush each crescent with remaining fruit.

3. Bake 11–13 minutes or until golden; remove from baking sheet with spatula immediately. Serve warm.

Per serving:
Calories: 130   Fat: 7 g   Sodium: 237 mg   Protein: 2 g
Carbohydrate: 16 g   Cholesterol: 0 mg
Diabetic exchanges:
Starch/Bread: 0.67   Fat: 1.25   Fruit: 0.33

Lemon–Poppy Seed Mini Tea Muffins

Makes 24 muffins.
These tiny muffins are the perfect tea accompaniments.

- 2 tablespoons unsalted butter
- 2 tablespoons margarine
- 1/4 cup unsweetened pineapple juice concentrate
- 1/4 cup plain nonfat yogurt
- 1 large egg
- 1 teaspoon lemon extract
- 1 cup unbleached all-purpose flour
- 2 tablespoons poppy seeds
- 1/2 teaspoon each baking soda and baking powder
- 1/2 teaspoon grated lemon zest
- 1/4 teaspoon salt

1. Preheat oven to 400°F; spray 24 mini muffin-pan cups with vegetable cooking spray; set aside.

2. In large bowl of electric mixer, cream butter and margarine at medium speed; add juice concentrate, yogurt, egg, and extract; beat 3 minutes, scraping down sides of bowl.

3. In medium bowl combine flour, poppy seeds, baking soda, baking powder, lemon zest, and salt; with mixer at low speed gradually add to butter mixture until just blended.

4. Divide batter evenly among muffin cups. Bake 20–25 minutes or until toothpick inserted in center comes out clean; turn onto rack to cool.

Per serving:
Calories: 52   Fat: 3 g   Sodium: 64 mg   Protein: 1 g
Carbohydrate: 6 g   Cholesterol: 11 mg

Diabetic exchanges:
Starch/Bread: 0.33   Fat: 0.50

Madeleines

Makes 24.
These French sweets are plump little cakes resembling sea shells.
They are traditionally spongy and meant to be "dunked" in tea.

   2 large eggs
   1/4 cup pineapple spreadable fruit
   1 teaspoon lemon extract
   1 cup unbleached all-purpose flour
   1/2 teaspoon baking powder
   Pinch salt
   1/2 cup reduced-calorie tub margarine, melted and
        cooled

1. Preheat oven to 375°F; spray two 12-shell madeleine
   pans with vegetable cooking spray; set aside.

2. In large bowl, with mixer at high speed, beat eggs, fruit
   spread, and lemon extract until thick and creamy, about
   10 minutes.

3. In small bowl combine flour, baking powder, and salt; sift
   about 1/4 cup at a time over egg mixture; fold until
   blended. Fold in margarine all at once until blended.

4. Fill shells 3/4 full. Bake about 15 minutes until brown
   around edges. Turn onto rack to cool.

Per serving:
Calories: 50   Fat: 2 g   Sodium: 56 mg   Protein: 1 g
Carbohydrate: 6 g   Cholesterol: 18 mg
Diabetic exchanges:
Starch/Bread: 0.33   Fat: 0.50

Pecan Tea Loaves

Makes 2 small loaves or 8 servings.
Not too sweet tea loaves with a hint of orange flavor. Serve with unsweetened orange marmalade. These loaves can be frozen, and make perfectly dainty gifts.

    13/4 cups unbleached all-purpose flour
    1/4   cup chopped pecans
    1   teaspoon baking soda
    1/4   teaspoon salt
    1/2   cup unsweetened orange juice concentrate
    3   tablespoons vegetable oil
    2   large eggs
    1   tablespoon orange marmalade spreadable fruit
    1   teaspoon vanilla extract
    1/2   teaspoon orange extract

1. Preheat oven to 350°F; spray two 6-×3 1/2-inch loaf pans with vegetable cooking spray; set aside.

2. In large bowl combine dry ingredients; in small bowl combine remaining ingredients; add liquid ingredients to dry, stirring until just blended.

3. Spoon batter evenly into loaf pans; bake 25–30 minutes or until toothpick inserted in center comes out clean.

4. Cool on rack 5 minutes; remove from pans and cool completely.

Per serving:
Calories: 224   Fat: 9 g   Sodium: 187 mg   Protein: 5 g
Carbohydrate: 30 g   Cholesterol: 53 mg

Diabetic exchanges:
Starch/Bread: 1.50   Fat: 1.75   Fruit: 0.50

Whole Wheat Zucchini Bread

Makes 1 loaf or 12 servings.
A healthy and tasty quick bread.

- 1 1/2 cups whole wheat flour
- 1 teaspoon baking soda
- 1/2 teaspoon salt
- 1/2 teaspoon each ground cinnamon and allspice
- 1/2 cup vegetable oil
- 1/4 cup unsweetened apple juice concentrate
- 1 large egg + 2 egg whites
- 3 tablespoons peach spreadable fruit
- 2 teaspoons vanilla extract
- 1 1/2 cups shredded zucchini (about 1 medium)

1. Preheat oven to 350°F; spray 9- × 5-inch loaf pan with vegetable cooking spray; set aside.

2. In large bowl combine dry ingredients; in medium bowl combine oil, juice concentrate, egg, egg whites, fruit spread, and vanilla extract. Pour liquid ingredients into dry and stir until just blended. Fold in zucchini.

3. Pour into prepared pan. Bake 45–55 minutes or until toothpick inserted in center comes out clean. Cool on rack 10 minutes; remove from pan and cool completely.

Per serving:
Calories: 166   Fat: 10 g   Sodium: 177 mg   Protein: 3 g
Carbohydrate: 16 g   Cholesterol: 18 mg
Diabetic exchanges:
Starch/Bread: 1.00   Fat: 2.00

8

Frozen Desserts

Blackberry-Peach Sherbet

Makes 6 servings.
The use of frozen fruits makes this a year-round dessert.

- 2 cups frozen blackberries
- 2 cups frozen peaches
- 1/4 cup unsweetened pineapple juice concentrate
- 2 tablespoons finely chopped fresh mint (1 1/2 teaspoons dried)
- 2 tablespoons peach spreadable fruit

Mint leaves to garnish

1. In food processor fitted with steel blade, combine all ingredients; pulse until blended.

2. Pour into 8-inch pan. Cover and freeze until firm, about 4 hours.

3. Spoon ice into medium bowl of electric mixer (not a food processor); beat until smooth at medium speed.

4. Place sherbet in a freezer container and freeze until ready to serve. Scoop into dessert dishes and garnish with mint leaves.

Per serving:
Calories: 85   Fat: <1 g   Sodium: <1 g   Protein: 1 g
Carbohydrate: 21 g   Cholesterol: 0 mg
Diabetic exchange:
Fruit: 1.50

Buttermilk-Mango Sherbet

Makes 4 servings.
Mangoes, originally from India, are now cultivated around the world. The contrast of sweet mangoes and slightly sour buttermilk are a perfect combination in this creamy sherbet.

- 1   cup low-fat buttermilk
- 1   large egg
- 2   teaspoons vanilla extract
- 2   small ripe mangoes (about 2 pounds), peeled, pitted, and sliced
- 2   tablespoons peach spreadable fruit

1. In small saucepan, over low heat, combine buttermilk and egg; cook 5 minutes, whisking constantly. Remove from heat; add vanilla; refrigerate until cold, about 1 hour.

2. In blender or food processor, puree remaining ingredients; add buttermilk mixture until well blended.

3. Pour mixture into container of ice-cream machine and follow manufacturer's instructions.

4. Transfer to freezer container; place in freezer to harden. For easy serving, soften in refrigerator 30 minutes.

Per serving:
Calories: 173   Fat: 2 g   Sodium: 83 mg   Protein: 4 g
Carbohydrate: 36 g   Cholesterol: 56 mg
Diabetic exchanges:
Dairy, Skim Milk: 0.25   Fat: 0.50   Fruit: 2.00

Cherry-Banana Ice Pops

Makes 6 pops.
A sweet ice pop that's fun for big and little kids alike!

    2   medium-size ripe bananas, sliced
    1 1/4 cups unsweetened mountain cherry juice
    1   tablespoon fresh lemon juice

1. Place all ingredients in blender container; process until smooth.

2. Pour mixture evenly into six 7-ounce paper cups.

3. Place in freezer 45 minutes; stir mixture in each cup.

4. Freeze an additional 45 minutes or until semi-solid; insert a wooden stick into center of each cup. When frozen, cover with plastic wrap.

5. To serve, let paper cups stand at room temperature for 10 minutes; peel away cups.

Per serving:
Calories: 61   Fat: <1 g   Sodium: 4 mg   Protein: .39 g
Carbohydrate: 15 g   Cholesterol: 0 mg
Diabetic exchange:
Fruit: 1.00

Creamed Papaya Frozen Tofu

Makes 6 servings.
This delicious creamy nondairy dessert is very close to ice cream in texture.

21/4 cups (16 ounces) mashed drained tofu
1   cup unsweetened creamed papaya juice concentrate*
1/2 cup pineapple spreadable fruit**
1   teaspoon vanilla extract
Pinch of salt

1. In food processor fitted with steel blade, combine all ingredients; process until smooth.

2. Place mixture into container of ice-cream machine and follow manufacturer's instructions for frozen yogurt.

3. If not serving immediately, transfer to freezer container. For easy serving, soften in refrigerator 30 minutes.

Per serving:
Calories: 183   Fat: 4 g   Sodium: 35 mg   Protein: 6 g
Carbohydrate: 34 g   Cholesterol: 0 mg
Diabetic exchanges:
Meat, Med.: 0.75   Fruit: 2.25

---

* Available at health food stores.
** Variation: 1 cup pureed fruit of choice and spreadable fruit to taste.

Espresso Granita

Makes 6 servings.
Granita is a coarser-grained ice than sorbet. Although a favorite in the test kitchen, this dessert is not recommended for those who like their coffee very sweet.

- 2 cups brewed espresso coffee, cooled and refrigerated
- 1/4 cup anisette or Sambuca liqueur
- 1/2 teaspoon vanilla extract
- 1/2 teaspoon grated lemon zest

1. In 4-cup measure combine all ingredients; pour mixture into an 8-inch-square metal pan. Cover and freeze 2 hours.

2. Spoon mixture in large bowl of electric mixer; beat at medium speed until fluffy, 4–6 minutes. Spoon into covered freezer container; freeze overnight. For easy serving, soften in refrigerator 30 minutes.

Per serving:
Calories: 30   Fat: 0 g   Sodium: 2 mg   Protein: .07 g
Carbohydrate: 3 g   Cholesterol: 0 mg
Diabetic exchanges:
Fat: 0.50   Fruit: 0.20

Frozen Banana-Cinnamon Yogurt

Makes 8 servings.
This very low-fat treat is creamy when served immediately but slightly more flavorful when frozen for a few hours.

    5   cups plain nonfat yogurt
    1   medium-size ripe banana, mashed
    1/2 cup pineapple–orange–banana juice concentrate
    1   teaspoon each vanilla and banana extract
    1/2 teaspoon ground cinnamon

1. In large bowl combine all ingredients; refrigerate 1 hour.

2. Pour mixture into container of ice-cream machine and follow manufacturer's instructions. If not serving immediately, transfer to freezer container. For easy serving, soften in refrigerator 30 minutes.

Per serving:
Calories: 125   Fat: <1 g   Sodium: 110 mg   Protein: 9 g
Carbohydrate: 22 g   Cholesterol: 3 mg
Diabetic exchanges:
Dairy, Skim Milk: 0.75   Fruit: 0.75

Strawberry Ice Milk

Makes 12 servings.
Use the sweetest, ripest strawberries available for this creamy confection.

- 1½ cups 1% low-fat milk
- 1½ cups sliced, hulled strawberries
- ⅓ cup strawberry pourable fruit
- ¼ cup low-fat plain yogurt
- ⅛ teaspoon ground cinnamon

1. Combine all ingredients in blender container; process until smooth.

2. Pour mixture into container of ice-cream machine and follow manufacturer's instructions. If not serving immediately, transfer to freezer container. For easy serving, soften in refrigerator 30 minutes.

Per serving:
Calories: 37   Fat: <1 g   Sodium: 24 mg   Protein: 1 g
Carbohydrate: 7 g   Cholesterol: 2 mg
Diabetic exchanges:
Dairy, Skim Milk: 0.13   Fruit: 0.33

Tortoni (Almond Ice Milk)

Makes 8 servings.
Inspired by frozen almond cream served in little paper cups in neighborhood Southern Italian restaurants.

- 2 cups 1% low-fat milk
- 1/3 cup peach spreadable fruit
- 1 teaspoon each almond and vanilla extract
- 2 tablespoons toasted sliced almonds, coarsely chopped
- 2 tablespoons toasted unsweetened coconut to garnish, optional

1. In 4-cup measure or blender combine milk, fruit spread, and extracts until blended.

2. Pour into container of ice-cream machine and process, following manufacturer's instructions. Stir in almonds.

3. Divide mixture evenly into 8 doubled cupcake-papers; sprinkle with coconut and freeze on tray. When frozen, cover with foil. Refrigerate 30 minutes before serving.

Per serving:
Calories: 66   Fat: 1 g   Sodium: 31 mg   Protein: 2 g
Carbohydrate: 10 g   Cholesterol: 2 mg
Diabetic exchanges:
Dairy, Skim Milk: 0.25   Fat: 0.25   Fruit: 0.50

Watermelon Sorbet

Makes 6 servings.
A fine-textured ice. Cassis deepens the color of this summer treat.

- 4 cups cubed seeded watermelon
- 1/2 cup unsweetened white grape juice
- 2 tablespoons cassis liqueur, optional

1. In food processor fitted with steel blade, puree watermelon; add grape juice, cassis, and 1/2 cup water; process to combine.

2. Pour mixture into container of ice-cream machine and follow manufacturer's instructions.

3. If not serving immediately, transfer to freezer container. For easy serving, soften in refrigerator 30 minutes.

Per serving:
Calories: 47   Fat: <1 g   Sodium: 4 mg   Protein: <1 g
Carbohydrate: 11 g   Cholesterol: 0 mg
Diabetic exchange:
Fruit: 0.75

Index

About the Author

Linda Romanelli Leahy is former test-kitchen director for *Weight Watchers Magazine* and a professional recipe developer with a special interest and expertise in baking. She is the critically acclaimed author of *The Oat Bran Cookbook* and the soon-to-be-published *The Universal Peanut Butter Cookbook.*